The author was born in Tehran, Iran. He moved to Germany to study at the University of Hamburg. Dr Dariush obtained his doctorate degree there in economics and politics, then stopped writing scientific articles for universities and institutes and entered the world of business.

This book is dedicated to Angelika for her kindness of heart.

Dr Dariush Pourkian

FIVE YEARS LIVING IN ELAHIYEH, FERESHTEH STREET

AUSTIN MACAULEY PUBLISHERS™
LONDON • CAMBRIDGE • NEW YORK • SHARJAH

Copyright © Dr Dariush Pourkian 2024

The right of Dr Dariush Pourkian to be identified as the author of this work has been asserted by the author in accordance with sections 77 and 78 of the Copyright, Designs and Patents Act 1988.

All rights reserved. No part of this publication may be reproduced, stored in a retrieval system, or transmitted in any form or by any means, electronic, mechanical, photocopying, recording, or otherwise, without the prior permission of the publishers.

Any person who commits any unauthorised act in relation to this publication may be liable to criminal prosecution and civil claims for damages.

All of the events in this memoir are true to the best of author's memory. The views expressed in this memoir are solely those of the author.

A CIP catalogue record for this title is available from the British Library.

ISBN 9781035838752 (Paperback)
ISBN 9781035838769 (ePub e-book)

www.austinmacauley.com

First Published 2024
Austin Macauley Publishers Ltd®
1 Canada Square
Canary Wharf
London
E14 5AA

I wish to express my special gratitude to Minou Alian for the translation of this book.

Preface

The present edition is the continuation of the book *The Battered Generation*, which covered the years 1953-1958, when I was living in Elahiyeh, Shemiran, with my family. During those years, I was gradually leaving my childhood behind and entering my adolescence. At that time, I closely watched my parents' behaviour and how they treated others and assessed their character. What my father did at home and outside was not always acceptable to me. Sometimes, I considered them immoral, rude and even unfair.

However, I was careful not to offend him with my words and didn't want him to think I was a rebellious child. I always talked very formally with him and never forgot to address him with the word "Shoma" instead, which is the polite word used in Persian when talking with the elders and superiors. The link between us was mostly my mother, who conveyed my wishes, annoyance, joy and even ideas to my father, like a messenger.

One day, as my complaints to my mother about my father's way of life grew, he felt the need to talk to me. So, as he was planting a tree in the garden below our own, he told me: 'If we want to be fair in our judgement of the people, we've got to know that the society is made up of two groups only; the lambs and the wolves. Lambs are always killed and preyed on, while the wolves devour and move forward.'

Then he asked me: 'Which group do you want to belong to? Lambs or wolves?'

At first, I was confused by this sudden question. After thinking for a while, I replied: 'Something between a lamb and a wolf.'

He answered that it was not possible as there is no other group than these two and then continued: 'If you fall short in the community and act mercifully, you'll be eaten and lost.'

It was at this point that I came to understand the reason for my father's actions and behaviour and why he was sometimes harsh and rude in his dealings with others but considerate at other times. He also insisted that he treated the others very gently. He told me that I had to see what some of his friends do mercilessly to achieve their goals, even by walking on the corpses of the others. I just realised that what my father meant was this constant war and quarrel happening between human beings.

My purpose in writing this book is only to record the events and things that I've witnessed with my own eyes. Perhaps they can be thought of as social history. I haven't tried much to match the names of the streets in those years with their present names, as they have been changed a few times.

This book consists of two parts. In the first part, I've covered the description of the location of Elahiyeh and its surroundings and even beyond its limits before dealing with the details of my place of residence to show the reader what the area looked like in my time. They are in fact my own personal observations, experiences and evaluations during my stay in those years which might not be perfect. So I'd be glad to receive any comments and opinions sent to me. My contact phone number and email address are as follows:

>Phone: 004940446615
>Email: *d.pourkian@yahoo.com*

In the second part, I describe my five years of residence on Fereshteh Street in Elahiyeh, with the aim of showing a part of Iranian family life with all its problems, joys and shortcomings.

I also thank my family and friends, Mohammad Alizadeh, a classmate and my teacher, Amir Biglarbeigi, who helped and advised me in writing this book.

Building a House in Elahiyeh, Fereshteh Street and Moving into It

My father, Mohammad, was a fun-loving man. He hadn't seen Elahiyeh before. While we were still living on "Rah Ahan" in the southern section of Tehran, he heard from a friend who told him one Friday: 'Let's go to Elahiyeh to have a nice time.'

My father asked where the place was, and he said: 'I'll show it to you.'

At that time, Mohammad had a Ford car of that small model which was imported by Mrs Fakhr al-Dowleh.

The first taxis in Tehran were those of Fords. So, going left and right, he took Mohammad right to the brook running from the Qanat where we later built our house. Water flowed from the ground next to our future home. There were old walnut, mulberry and sycamore trees behind the land and next to the street.

They spread a blanket on the ground under the trees and put their picnic goodies on it. There was no one there. Then they started eating the cold turkey's leg with lemon juice, bread and Olivier salad and talked about their sweet memories.

Mohammad was thinking to himself: *What a cosy and serene place it is. It's nice to buy a piece of land here by the running water and build a house on it. The air is so cool and fresh here.*

Elahiyeh was located right on the route to the Tochal resort area. I enjoyed real cool air in summer. Meanwhile, a shepherd appeared to graze his herd in the afternoon. Mohammad asked him who the land belonged to.

The shepherd said: 'To Mrs Fakhr al-Dowleh.'

Mohammad wondered how she'd come to own that place. I later found out that she'd inherited that land from her ancestors and not bought it. Mohammad was lucky that day not to be disturbed by anyone. Apparently, a gang of rubbers took ransom from those who'd come on a picnic to that place.

Elahiyeh was a place to go to for fun. Young people didn't have much freedom at that time. If they wanted to take their girlfriend or a woman somewhere, they came to the wheat fields of Elahiyeh and made love among the trees. There were, however, some people who'd disturb them. The gang was run by N. S. who was a tall and brave bully.

Together with K. S., V. S. and A. M., they caught those who came to Elahiyeh and asked for ransom, saying: 'You've come here to our property to make love with people's daughter and should pay for it.'

This had become some kind of fun for them. The German Ambassador was passing through there to "Pol-e Rumi" one day. Apparently, he was charmed by the poetic beauty of the area and had stopped to look at it. The gang even stopped the German Ambassador and asked him for money. They were arrested a few days later and put in jail.

With his power and authority, Mrs Fakhr al-Dowleh's son, Ali Amini, ordered the place to be watched and guarded.

The next morning, Mohammad went to the palace of Mrs Fakhr al-Dowleh. He asked his agent, Modarressi, about the land where the water of the Qanat passed through, but Modarressi didn't know much about it. So, a few days later, Mohammad went to Mrs Fakhr al-Dowleh herself and told her that if she gave that land to him, he'd also sell the other surrounding lands at a good price for her. Pleased with this offer, she asked him to promise, and he did. Mohammad told her that he planned to build a house on that land and settle there.

Then Mohammad sent an engineer there to determine the location of that land. Meanwhile, Mrs Fakhr al-Dowleh called the registrar of the documents. They finally said that the land intended by Mohammad was 1,500 sq. m. Mrs Fakhr al-Dowleh sold that land to Mohammad at 10 Ts/m.

Through his dealings with Mrs Fakhr al-Dowleh, Mohammad got to know her as an energetic, intelligent, disciplined, very materialistic and intellectual woman with strong discernment and correct judgement. This is how he described her character to my mother.

Photo No. 1: Taken from Amaniyeh Hill, Elahiyeh area, in front of the planted trees of Vojdani St, which led to Taraz Garden. Fereshteh Street is located at the left end of the dense trees. Our future homeland is on the left, which is not seen in the photo, but the dense trees in the middle of the photo on the left are located behind the back of our future home (10 August 1951).

Mrs Fakhr al-Dowleh's own house with a garden was approximately 100,000 square metres. At that time, this was written on the door of her house: "Mrs Fakhr al-Dowleh's Nest". Whenever Mohammad passed by it, he kicked its wall out of anger because she'd built a 100,000 square metre house and called it a nest. She probably expected her house to cover the entire Iran.

Upon buying the land, Mohammad started building a wall with green stones around it, planned by himself. Then he built a house and a garden there. Next, as promised, he began to sell some of Mrs Fakhr al-Dowleh's land. The price of Fereshteh lands later reached 300 Tumans per metre.

Photo No. 2: Mrs Fakhr al-Dowleh at the age of about 60.

Mohammad wasn't an engineer and had no experience in building. Prior to World War II, he had built a few houses under the supervision of his engineer friend, Misaqi. However, his role in that construction at that time was mainly in investing, doing office work and hiring the architect and construction workers. Now, in addition to his daily work, he was in charge of building the house and constantly monitored the progress of the building and dealt with the workers during the week.

When the weather was warm, once every week or two, Mohammad took us to Elahiyeh with his friends and family. There were old walnut trees on the east side, behind the wall of the house, where we spread a few blankets topped with a tablecloth and spent the holidays with barbecue, rice, salads and drinks. We were so happy with these gatherings that neither we nor the other guests paid any attention to our future home and life in that area. What was just interesting for us was dancing and singing and having tea from the samovar and eating lunch together.

When the construction of Elahiyeh house took the minimum living conditions standard and was ready for us to move in, Mohammad gave a great party. He invited everyone in the family, along with the family of his close friend Taraz and other friends. They spread the blankets there under the trees as usual to sit on and slaughtered a sheep.

The workers salted and seasoned the sheep without chopping it and turned it on a big fire from a large brazier that they'd made with wood and iron. When it was fully roasted, they chopped it into pieces and placed it on a large tray. Rice was also cooked inside the house and placed on the tablecloth.

After lunch, my aunt Maryam's husband, Mohammad Ali, started playing happy music on his "Tar" accompanied by Maryam playing the tambourine. Those who knew how to dance got up, including my other aunt Turan, my mother and even my father. Others accompanied them with applause. Then we walked around the house together and took a few souvenir pictures.

Photo No. 3: Sitting from front to left: Ahmad, my uncle, Nezam, Taraz's third son, Taraz, Taraz's wife, Dr Khal`ati, Zari Khanum's husband, Sanam, Delshad, Zari Khanum, Maryam's maid, Hajar, our servant Nasser, unknown, Dariush, Kourosh, unknown woman clapping, Iran. Standing from right to left: Taraz's second son, Kouros, Mohammad Ali playing the "Tar", an unknown lady, Maryam playing the tambourine, Mohammad and Turan clapping and my mother, Ashraf, dancing (early summer, 1953).

Photo No. 4: Sitting from right to left: our servant, Nasser, my uncle, Ahmad, with his back to the photographer, my father's friend, Taraz, Dr Khal`ati, Sanam, Zari Khanum, unknown boy, unknown lady with kerchief, Hajar, Maryam's maid, unknown lady with scarf, unknown. In front of her Vida, others unknown, Dariush back to the photographer. Standing from right to left: Mohammad dancing, Maryam playing the tambourine that's not seen in the photo, Mohammad Ali with his "Tar" (early summer, 1953).

Photo No. 5: Under Amaniyeh Hill, Vojdani St leading to Taraz Garden from afar. Front row from right to left: Siranoush, Bahram and Dariush in striped pants. Second row from right to left: unknown boy, Kouros, Maryam, Turan, unknown, Taraz's wife, my mother, Ashraf, unknown, Iran, Zari Khanum, Taraz's wife's maid, Vida. Third row from right to left: Mehran, Maryam's son, Mehran, in Delshad's arms (the babysitter), Hajar, Maryam's other maid (early summer, 1953).

Photo No. 6: At the foot of Amaniyeh Hill. Vojdani St is seen on the right side that leads to Taraz's garden at the back of the picture. First row sitting from right to left: Kouros, Nezam, Dariush, unknown boy, Kourosh, unknown girl, unknown girl, Siranoush, Bahram. Second row: Mehran in Delshad's arms (the babysitter), unknown boy and girl. Standing in the first row from right to left: Taraz's wife's maid, Zari Khanum, Maryam's maid, Hajar, my mother, Ashraf, unknown, Taraz's wife, unknown lady, Sanam, Iran and Mahmoud. Third row from right to left: Maryam's maid, Hajar, Taraz and Hesam, his third son, Maryam's husband, Mohammad Ali, my father, Mohammad, an unknown person behind Mohammad (early summer 1953).

The day of moving arrived at last. Our former house was located in the "Rah Ahan" area almost 300 metres away from the square. It was a Friday afternoon in late August 1953 when we started from "Rah Ahan" towards Shemiran, in the northern section of Tehran. There were my father and his errand boy, Mashallah, my mother and baby Kourosh in her arms, me and Siranoush, my sister, who helped the driver load everything in his truck. It was said in those days that the rich moved by truck and the poor by cart. But we weren't rich.

Next to the driver, in front of the truck, sat Ashraf, Mohammad, Siranoush and Kourosh. Mashallah and I, tired of carrying the furniture, lay on the carpets at the back of the truck and watched the cars behind, the trees on both sides of the road and the surrounding scenery as we drove. We passed through Amiriyeh and Moniriyeh Streets and Shah Reza intersection (now Enqelab) and entered the north Pahlavi Road (now Valiasr).

I noticed the freshwater on both sides of the street running by the beautiful sycamore trees. Mohammadi rose bushes, which were native flowers with four petals, were planted in between the trees. Some people dried the petals and poured them into yoghurt drinks to make them fragrant. Roses had several pests like bugs and spider webs and the leaves oxidised quickly. To remove them, they washed the petals with soap and water or treat them with the juice of the leaves of the tree of heaven or nettle juice.

Photo No. 7: Pahlavi Road (now Valiasr) in 1950.

We were moving on a narrow, two-lane and asphalt road where only two cars could pass each other. The road needed a little repair. The distance between the asphalt road and the creek was still dirt. After 19 August 1953, the dirt distance was asphalted and added to the main road, thus widening the road from Tehran to Tajrish. However, from Tajrish, in front of the "Goushvareh Talai" restaurant, they started the widening operation towards the south.

"Goushvareh Talai" (or Golden earring) was owned later on by "Delkash", a female radio singer. Thus the joke was told among people that said: 'This time, the state has started the work from the top because there has always been oppression at the bottom.' Pahlavi Road was built by the order of Reza Shah to be a link between Sa'ad Abad Palace in

Tajrish and the royal palaces on Pahlavi Street and Kakh Street behind the Senate. In other words, they were the summer and winter quarters of the court.

There were several palaces in that area that constituted the Shah's office and the Royal Family residence. As long as Reza Shah was in Iran, Pahlavi Road was almost a private road up to Abshar (Waterfall) station and No. 2 Army Hospital. No one had the right to travel further than that on that road. It was only for the Pahlavi dynasty (court), dignitaries and foreign ambassadors and guests. Ordinary people used to go to Shemiran from the old road. It later became public.

We left the city. The truck was now heading uphill to the north. I looked around well. Everything was new to me. Dry hills and barren lands on my right and left-hand side caught my attention. Small huts appeared occasionally on the right-hand side of the road, between the plains and the desert.

Not far from Army Hospital No. 2, on the right of the Pahlavi Road (Present Valiasr), there was an Armenian settlement. Some scrapped and broken-down trucks belonging to the US military that had survived the war and the Allied withdrawal from Iran were still there and had not been returned to the United States. A person named Ardakani had bought them cheaply and sold their parts there. In front of it, there was the brook water of Karaj on the left side of the Pahlavi Road.

As we came further up, we reached the Army Hospital No. 2 on the left-hand side of the road towards Shemiran, with a guarded wooden stall next to it. Right in front of the hospital, on the right of Pahlavi Road, there was a road that had a military aspect and went east from Pahlavi Street to the hills of Abbas Abad.

Passing the private mental hospital of Dr Seyyed Ebrahim Chehrazi and Dr Abdolhossein Mir Sepasi and the private zoo belonging to Dolatshahi, we passed the Amanieh Hill and reached Mahmoudieh station. The truck turned right there and entered Fereshteh Street (now Morteza Fayyazi) which was a dirt road slopping downwards.[1]

The truck moved downhill and slowed down. There were barren lands visible on the right-hand side of the street. Then a high hill appeared which was connected to higher hills on its south. On the left side of the street, there were a few large gardens with a dried-up river in between them. A bridge of almost 3 metres long accessed both sides of the river.

As we descended the hill, the slope decreased and we came to a junction. A dirt path on the right to the south passed through the hills at the back of Amanieh which was called Vojdani St (now Bidar). I later found out that the path led to the garden of my father's friend, Mr Taraz. The truck continued on its way.

The open road went down with a steep slope after about 50 metres. On the right side of the street, there were just gardens full of fruits which were enclosed by brick walls, by their owners. The dried-up river still continued on the left-

---

[1] It is said that there was no Fereshteh Street a few years earlier. It was all a hilly area with just a narrow dirt St going downwards. Fereshteh was the name of a girl favoured by Abbas Massoudi, the director of Ettela`at Newspaper. He had his house there, as you entered right from Pahlavi St, after the garden of Shapour Reporter (Ardeshir J.) on the left-hand side.

hand side. Getting about 800 metres away from Pahlavi St, on the slope after a few light turns, we reached an intersection and the truck braked and stopped right by the road.

We had reached our new home. It was called Elahiyeh where the rich people lived. Getting out of the truck, I looked around. There was only our house there to be seen. There were either wastelands or abandoned gardens around our house. There was a great distance, almost 200 metres, between our house and the next neighbour on our east on Fereshteh Street.

At the back of our house, beyond the walnut trees, there was a great plain that reached some hills on the south. After that, a row of sycamore trees could be seen that hid our neighbour's house next to the trees. For this reason, I never knew who lived in that house. My mother, sister and I were shocked by this unfavourable scene and wondered why our father had taken us to this desert wasteland. This wasn't a suitable place to live in; it was just good to spend the three summer months in that cool air.

There was still no electricity there, and consequently, it lacked access to electricity, radio and telephone and even proper drinking water. I heard my mother blaming our father for having taken us to that desert, to which my father quickly retorted: 'Thanks a lot! How thankful you are! I've taken you to an area full of vitamins in its air! Just breathe and refresh yourselves!' Then he turned his face to the garden and took a few deep breaths of that fresh and fragrant air with the scent of flowers and entered the garden house.[2]

The driver, Mohammad and Mashallah took the furniture home one by one. I, too, managed to take my own belongings

---

[2] A garden house is a house with a large garden.

inside. Thus we were the first group to enter that area. A green stone wall surrounded our new house and garden. Mohammad had left the stones there piled up with a lot of effort and expense, but their work was not over yet.

The house only had a large gate and an incomplete building in which they had to work with the workers in the same way. Even the garden was incomplete with no trees, bushes or flowers planted in it. Mohammad wanted to do the work little by little on the weekends after we moved in. Inside the house, it still smelt damp, and there were spiders in the bathroom.

The Location of Our Elahiyeh House

Our new house had a total area of 1,500 square metres. It consisted of two parts—the lower part was a 1,000 square metres of garden, and the one on top consisted of 200 square metres of a flat building and 300 square metres of garden.

A few weeks passed since we moved into our new home. Workers were still working inside our house. They filled the holes in between the green stones and covered all the gaps there. Everywhere smelt damp and muddy. In the first weeks, Mohammad himself worked hard in the lower backyard and the upper garden with the workers and showed them how to plot and plant the garden.

This is how our house looked like when the work was finished; entering the house on the north from the lower part, we first got into the garden. Then after 10 metres on the right, we climbed six steps and got into the porch and then the building. Our big kitchen was located next to the entrance door of the building. A 3 metres long corridor, on the right, joined the kitchen to the hall. Again, there was our restroom on the right-hand side, between the kitchen and the hall. There was a staircase next to it that led to the rooftop. There were three rooms around the hall. The left-hand side room on the east was our sitting room where "Nanneh Jan" (my mother's great-grandmother), Siranoush, Ashraf, my brother, Kourosh and I lived. After that, there was a small hallway connecting the hall to the east exit of the building.

Ashraf and Mohammad's bedroom was located on the left-hand side of the corridor. It also served as Mohammad's office. The balcony was on the south of the building. There was also another room on the east of the hall which was kept empty. We didn't have beds and slept on mattresses put on the floor. There was a large dining table in the centre of the hall where we welcomed our guests and family and acquaintances.

Coming back from school in the evenings, Siranoush and I did our homework in the sitting room. After eating dinner, Siranoush put her head on Nanneh Jan's lap and I put my head on her other one, and she told us sweet stories. Meanwhile, she'd start coughing hard because she was a smoker. Siranoush kept on telling her why she wouldn't keep telling the story, to which she'd reply with her Gilaki accent: 'This coughing doesn't let me talk, dear.'

Our tall, black heater on the other side of the room, with a kettle filled with water on top, kept us and our room warm in winter.

Water Supply in Our House

Water in our house was supplied from a reservoir in the upper yard built under the porch. Mohammad paid 20 Tumans to the man in charge of Amanieh Hill to divert water into our reservoir. Then he told me to use the Fakhr al-Dowleh water, which came from their big garden stream several times a week and flowed down by our house on Fereshteh Street, to irrigate the lower garden.

There were three Qanats in our area: "Galaab", meaning muddy water, "Dakion" and "Fakhr al-Dowleh" which was the only one that reached Elahieh. It flowed from Mrs Fakhr al-Dowleh's property and passed in front of Shapur High School (now Jalal Al Ahmad). There, it was pumped up to irrigate the surrounding gardens, including ours. Mrs Fakhr al-Dowleh sold this water to the orchardists and the neighbours in the lower part of Fereshteh Street. The Qanat was dredged every few years to give a proper slope to the running water.

Nourian was the man in charge of Fakhr al-Dowleh Qanat who also had other duties in her organisation. After his death, his son, Majid, took charge of his duties. He was known as "Majid Siah", Black Majid, due to his dark complexion. His office was located in a circle on Fereshteh Street which was later called "Fereshteh Square". This square was about 300 metres away from our house towards "Pol-e-Rumi".

Later on, due to more building constructions in Elahieh which demanded more water supply, Mrs Fakhr al-Dowleh dug a deep well at the top of what is now known as Mahmoud Hesabi Street, parallel to the upper east of Kazemi Street (now Takhti Street), where the houses of General Razmara, General Amir Ahmadi, Commander Shaghaghi, Commander Haji Nouri, Haj Naghi Kashani and one side of the house of Dr Namdar were located. She also sold its water. Therefore, the water passed by our house most of the time. What we did then was probably not right, but Mohammad said that it was easier to irrigate the trees and vegetables in our garden from that water, without having to go to the upper yard for water.

Photo No. 8: Ms Fakhr al-Douleh in her late sixties, allegedly with one of her sons, a symbol of her efforts to irrigate her property and sell water to others, photo taken from "Modern History of Iran".

Planting Trees and Flowers in Our House

Mohammad, himself, started planting the trees one by one. He also asked me to hold the seedlings for him to strengthen the base. Then, on the same slope between the entrance gate and the stairs, he started a rose border with different colours alongside the wall. Above, in front of the large porch of the building, in the eastern part, he plotted a row of a garden where he sowed the seeds of daisies of different colours.

In the upper courtyard on the other side of the building to the south, Mohammad first planted small boxwoods next to the gardens. Then around them, he planted zinnias, nasturtiums, petunias, roses, snapdragons in different colours and blue, yellow, crimson and brown pansies, as well as pink and white oleanders which they said caused nose bleeding if smelled. Carnations, gladiola and geraniums were also added to that collection.

After a while, Mohammad started grafting rose bushes so that the flowers would have better colours and smells. It was as if my father had achieved his dream of building a chic greenhouse in his home. He asked me to water the seedlings and flowers of the garden and the garden of the upper courtyard in the mornings and evenings, and their number was increasing every day. I wasn't always happy to water them as it wasted one to one and a half hours of my time and deprived me of reading my favourite books and magazines which I'd just gotten accustomed to.

I was angry about that. I was even gradually getting allergic to all the trees and flowers I saw. I hated them for many years. The rest of the summer was spent planting trees. Everyone who came to our house was amazed by all the colourful flowers. The garden above our house was full of flowers.

Photo No. 9. Mohammad (author's father) at the age of 39, 1955.

After a while, Mohammad noticed that the garden needed a gardener to take care of it because of the large number of trees, flowers and vegetables he had planted in it. There were a lot of fruit trees, tomatoes, strawberries and other veggies growing there. So he hired a man named Valiollah, from Najaf Abad in Isfahan, and let him live in the room on the west side of the hall.

With the arrival of autumn, our work started again. Now we had to plant the cuttings of flowers, like geraniums, in soil, to protect them from the cold in winter. Their flowers were mostly red, pink and white in colour. We took all those large and rectangular pots, in which cuttings and flowers were planted, to the hall and rooms to keep them warm. Mohammad, himself, did all the work on Fridays or even in the middle of the week.

Valiollah and I helped him to take the pots inside and water them. Due to his hard work in the garden, Mohammad got terrible scars on his hands that hurt him a lot. Apparently, wearing gardening gloves was not yet common at that time. I think his hands were infected with fungus because after a few weeks of gardening, he received medical care for a few weeks and applied ointments and a special cream to them at night and covered them with a piece of cloth.

The Story of Lotfollah Taraqi and Mohammad's Black Rose

With his upper and lower gardens, Mohammad's love for flowers and seedlings increased so much that whenever he saw an interesting flower or seedling, he immediately bought it and planted it in his garden. One day, he came home with a bare-rooted sapling. He planted it in the garden in front of the building, on the east, and said: 'This is a rose bush that only bears black roses.'

I did not pay much attention to the meaning of his words because my interest and hobby was only in reading books, magazines and newspapers. The bush bloomed after a while, and I noticed that its flower was indeed a black rose.

One day, Mohammad took me to Lotfollah Taraqi, with himself. He was the publisher of the well-known magazines "Taraghi" and "Asia ye Javan" (Young Asia), a highly respected and influential man and an old close friend of my father. Lotfollah was a flower lover like Mohammad and planted the rarest flowers in his garden. Mohammad started talking and showing off his black rose. Maybe he wanted to make him jealous.

A few days later, Taraqi's gardener came to our house to see our black rose as he was told. The next day, he came back again to ask for the address of the place where Mohammad had got the plant from. At last, he said that he'd better dig out the bush and plant it in his master's garden as a gift since Mohammad could surely buy that bush again.

With an excuse, Mohammad returned him empty-handed. Two days later, on a Friday, Taraqi himself came to our house to see the much-praised rose by Mohammad and his gardener. It was interesting to me to see that Taraqi had come all that way to the end of Elahiyeh to see that black rose, despite his social rank and position in those days. He must have been in love with rare flowers, too.

Indirectly, he hinted to Mohammad to give him the bush as a gift. Mohammad entertained his old close friend nicely but returned him empty-handed. Later on, I never realised what happened to that rose, as it disappeared from our garden all of a sudden. Mohammad might have indeed given it to Lotfollah Taraqi as a gift. A black rose was one of those rare events occurring in nature which had great economic value. By cultivating and mass-producing it, it could be sold well, especially on the day of the death of the Prophet Mohammad, and the funeral rites.

My Amazements after Arriving in Elahiyeh

A twin-engine airplane flew over Elahiyeh sky every day and threw packs full of paper with interesting pictures on it. These small papers were the size of the palm of the hand, and their massive distribution in the air created a beautiful scene. Slowly dancing down, they landed on the hills and the ground. I think they were intended for the residents of Elahiyeh, as there were no television, radio or internet messages used to inform the people in those days. Those who had radios did not have electricity.

To inform the public, when necessary, they threw the messages by plane over the city and the countryside. I ran after every piece of these messages on the hills and plains, collected it all and took it home with me in batches. Different texts were written on these papers in different colours: "Long live the King", "Down with Mossaddeq", "Down with Tudeh Party" and "We wrote with our blood, Long live the King".

The situation hadn't returned to normal yet, after 19 August 1953. The government was trying to break the last resistance of the opposition with this kind of propaganda. On the occasion of the liberation of Azerbaijan, on 12 December 1946, that twin-engine plane was noticed again over Elahiyeh, handing out papers the size of a palm in the sky. They read: 'A strong army preserves our independence and makes every Iranian proud.'

A picture of the king, with the words of God Almighty on top of it, and the phrase "God, King, Iran" could be seen on it, which was apparently the slogan of the Iranian nation. Down, at the bottom left of the paper, it was written in small letters: "From the headquarters of Advertising and Publications".

While going to school from the end of Fereshteh Street (now Morteza Fayyazi), I'd slowly go uphill to Valiasr St. As there were very few cars moving on that street, with only a few seen from afar, I'd cross the street without fear and enter Mahmoudieh. Cars had a difficult time going up Valiasr Rd., in winter, on ice and snow. They didn't have much power. When a bus or a truck was coming up Amaniyeh Hill, they had to move with gear 1 or 2.

Their roar was heard from afar, moving slowly up the hill. When changing gears, big cars had to do it twice; they first put the gear in the neutral position, and then they pressed on the accelerator pedal and shifted to another gear. This action made a lot of noise.

Problems of Going to School for My Sister Siranoush and Me

My father, Mohammad, first registered Siranoush in a primary school near "Pol-e Rumi". She had to pass through the orchards on her way to get to school. The night following the day she'd been to school, my father asked her: 'How was the school today?'

She answered: 'School was fine and the way beautiful, but it's a little scary to go through the orchards alone.'

She was right. Generally speaking, living in that area was scary. Siranoush went to that school only one day because Mohammad got her out of there immediately and registered her at Mehr School in Tajrish. Then came winter. Heavy snow started falling, and her teachers were coming from Tehran. The school was disrupted because teachers weren't willing to come regularly, or they wouldn't come at all.

Consequently, kids rarely attended school. Siranoush, though, waited for teachers until noon, but no one would come. Therefore, she'd return home alone again. Siranoush and I were always in danger.

One afternoon, I left home for school. On my way, I came to a junction: One way to Vojdani Street under Amaniyeh Hill and Taraz Garden and the other one down to "Pol-e Rumi".

At that junction, I noticed a crazy driver constantly moving back and forth. When he saw me, he drove towards me quickly. This forced me to jump to the pavement and then towards Vojdani St. He got out of his car and cursed at me a few times.

Then he got back in his car and a few metres further, he started moving back and forth again. About a quarter of an hour later, Siranoush would come home that way. I told the story to my mother, but she didn't pay much attention to it. By the time Siranoush arrived, she said that she'd just seen such a car in the middle of the road, with a crazy driver wandering on the street.

Coming home from school for days, I would see the engineers at the same junction, measuring the height and the slope of the street and mapping the hill with their tripod engineering cameras. A few weeks later, the street was asphalted. The engineers or municipal employees did not seem to have enough experience or were embezzlers because they used little sand and gravel when paving. As a result, in the summer, shoes and wheels of cars and buses were tarred due to sinking into the asphalt, leaving their trace on the tar. The road was full of ups and downs due to the bad asphalt. Over time, however, they improved that street.

Bare and Naked Elahiyeh, Lacking Essential Living Standards

Before we moved to Elahiyeh where we lived, there were no facilities there for proper living; no shops, no electricity, no public baths and no doctors and mosques. Indeed, there was nothing there. People's shopping centre and dealing area were located in Hesabi Junction. There were two bakeries there at that time: One for "Sangak" (a type of Iranian bread) and the other for "Taftune" (another kind of bread in Iran). There were also a butchery, a carpentry, a mosque and at least four or five grocery stores there.

Hesabi Junction was where they distributed government sugar and a sugar cone. Haj Sha`ban's son, Mehdi Hamedi, was in charge of this distribution. This was a crowded area where poor workers and peasants lived. A few more stores opened in Mahmoudieh later on.

There were three class groups living in that area that were very different. One group was very rich. The children of some of them studied abroad. They had a garden in Elahiyeh, and it was a place of recreation and summer holidays for them. The second group were the natives of the area (Shemiran) whose main means of subsistence was through farming and keeping livestock (each had two cows and sold milk and its products), poultry and orchards which they sold its fruits in summer to fruit sellers in Sar-e Pol-e Tajrish and made money. The third group consisted of poor merchants, workers, carpenters, bricklayers and servants.

Lack of Electricity

In Elahiyeh, we did not have proper electricity in the beginning. The same oil lamps with bulbs and wicks were used at home. There were Petromax and paraffin lamps with good light, which were mostly used in shops but were not welcomed by the poor due to their high price.[3]

---

[3] In the beginning, in Tajrish, people had government electricity, which was called municipal electricity. Government electricity was weak, especially in summer when people came to Shemiran on holidays. As a result, consumption increased, and there was a shortage of electricity. Therefore, in that season, one side of the streets and alleys did not have electricity on odd days, and the other side on even days, until 9:00 and 10:00 pm. In other words, one side of the street had electricity one night, and the next night the other side could have it.

Kids were happy to listen to the radio or read and write their homework in the light of an electric lamp when they had electricity. Otherwise, oil lamps were used which were imported from Czechoslovakia. Iran itself produced oil lamps, too, but they were made of tin. In some families, active youngsters had a small transformer to listen to their radio when the power was off. These simple devices were made in Arak by young people.

They consisted of a coil in a box, two lamps, and glass pellets placed as a window. The only problem with these transformers was that

Elahiyeh Power Organisation was located on Fereshteh Street. If they wanted to cut off someone's electricity for some reason, they would go to that organisation.

Many houses still didn't have electricity because they were not included in the power limit and were out of the way of power lines. They had to use oil lamps for lightning. Those who had built themselves a new house, like us, had to apply for electricity and wait for several years for their turn to come.

Almost a year after our stay in Elahiyeh, "Tehran Power" came, and we got our electricity from them.

During the winter, snow settled on the power lines. Then, when it rained, they turned into icicle and caused the power lines to break. Wires fell on the street, creating a dangerous situation. Children collected and sold them by the metre for their pocket money. Or the families collected and used them as clotheslines.

---

they'd burn out when the power was high. You either had to turn off the device or turn off the power when the light was on. There was another simple way for low-cost lighting. They poured castor oil into a large bowl and placed a wick on it.

Then they lit it, and every half an hour or so, pulled up the wick a little. The lack of electricity, of course, did not include the nobility, the commanders, and the influential people in Shemiran. For the rich, on the nights when there was no electricity, they used the electricity from across the street. With a stick, they'd put the power cord of their house on the power cord on the other side of the street, or someone would go up the concrete beam of the light bulb, pick up the power cord and put it on the cord across the street.

Health Problem

Poor people in the area couldn't afford to pay 1 Tuman for the bath. And it wasn't common then to take a shower every day. Hygienic problem was more pronounced in winter, as children swam in pools and rivers in summer, or bathed in the stream water. In winter, however, it was a different issue. They had to wash themselves at home or in the public bath.

Because of this, when I was travelling by bus, the stench of some people on the bus bothered me very much. At school, I wouldn't notice it very much in class, as our noses were filled with different smells. It was reported that lice were running on the children's heads and faces in the first and second grades. The same thing was going on in Daihim School on Sa'ad Abad Street, by the King's palace.

In previous years, lice had caused people to get typhus. People used to get some powder from the health department and poured into clothes, especially children's sleeves and pants, to get rid of lice.

Hygiene was awkward. The soaps that were used then had a lot of caustic soda in them that got into the eyes and burnt them badly. My mother had a big sink in which she washed our clothes regularly.[4]

I often wondered where the poor washed themselves, especially in winter. They did not have enough money to go to the public bath. They used to "cat-wash" themselves at home, as the children of that time used to say. There were two public baths in our area—the "Haj Sayyah" bath at the beginning of Pahlavi Street at "Bagh Ferdos", which was open from five in the morning until nine at night, where our mother used to take us children for bathing. The other one which was named "Shazdeh Bath" that located at Hesabi Junction.

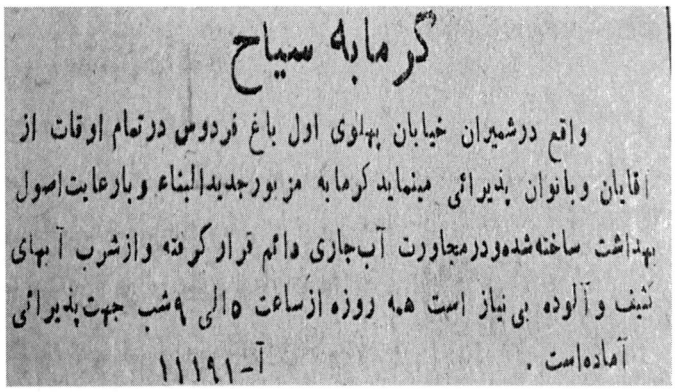

Photo No. 10: Ettela'at newspaper on the first Sunday of Azar 1332 (November 1953).

---

[4] Due to the existence of various dangerous diseases, especially typhoid fever, large pans were provided to the people at the location of the electricity department in the south of Tehran. People went there. They paid and boiled their underwear in those pans to kill the eggs of the lice.

I used to go to Haj Sayyah public bath on "Bagh Ferdos", on Fridays, with my father, or sometimes with my mother, every week. There were private family baths there. We took our turn and waited till we were called. There was a bathroom sign next to the bath counter which read: 'Whoever has something valuable with him should better hand it over to me at the time of arrival. Otherwise, if it is missed, I will not be responsible for it.'

Sometimes, it took over an hour and a half for our turn to come. There was a big clock on the wall in front of the counter that rang every 15 minutes. Wherever I heard a bell ring like that later on, I was immediately reminded of Sayyah public bath where we waited for our turn impatiently.

The hygiene that children were under pressure at school to learn, at the time, was not meant to be clean and stylish, but rather to have short nails, clean hands, face, ears and clothes.

Of course, by showing health movies, we kids learnt a lot.

In Search of Entertainment for Myself

We were living in a remote area without electricity, telephone, radio and sometimes even drinking water. Above it, all Siranoush and I had no one to play with. Whenever "Nanneh Jan" (my mother's grandmother) came to us, she said: 'Your dad has taken you to a desert valley and left you alone here.'

Being alone in Elahiyeh troubled us a lot. For my sister and I, who were still children, not having a playmate or classmate was painful. When family members like my uncle Mahmoud, who mostly played football with me, or Iran and Turan or Maryam (my aunts) came to visit us from the city, it was as if they had given us a world. We were very happy, but their departure was a disaster for us.

Siranoush and I both stood aside with a lump in the throat. We watched them with tears in our eyes and asked them to stay longer with us. Our eyes were our begging voices saying: 'Save us from this lonely world.'

In the evenings, I used to climb the Amaniyeh Hill or other nearby hills and, from there, watched the lights of the city of Tehran flickering.

Photo No. 11: Lonely graphics on the lower hill to the East of Amanieh Hill.

I envied those who lived in that city. Sometimes, if they showed a good play in the theatre in the city, Mohammad took us to the theatre, or we'd go to Lalehzar Street with my parents to buy clothes. Mohammad usually bought us clothes in the "General Mode" Store, or on upper Sa`di Street and in Lalehzar (Berlin Alley). He was probably impressed by the pretty advertisements of that store in newspapers that said: 'Both good and cheap, stylish and easy without spending a lot of time.'[5]

Sometimes, he bought our clothes from the "Pirayesh" Store in Lalehzar, near Iran Cinema, right across the street from Rex and Alborz cinemas.

---

[5] Ettela`at Newspaper, October 19, 1953, and May 2, 1956.

When it got warmer in May and June, I'd go around our house, alone or rarely with my school friends, to see where we were located and who owned which house or garden and what the landscape and nature looked like in that area.

During the day, my ears were filled with the sound of black crows, magpies with long tails and white breasts, sparrows and sometimes nightingales. My father said that magpies only lived in temperate climates. I later saw that my peers were hunting them. They said they stole rings and jewels. Our area was really a summer paradise.

There were only orchards, thick-trunked trees, small rural cottages and wheat and barley barns. At night, I heard the barking of the dogs of our distant neighbours. At dawn, the camels' bells, which went in caravans, caressed my ears. I'd never seen any other camels in that area except for once when there were no more than two or three of them going together. Maybe because I was still in bed at that time and it was too early to get up. I did not know where they came from and where they were going to and what they were carrying.

It was early summer and I was looking for entertainment. I had just got to know about the press. One of my hobbies was reading books. I also read "Taraqi", "Asia ye Javan" (Young Asia) and weekly "Ettela'at" magazines. Mohammad received the "Tarqi" magazine for free, due to his friendship with Lotfollah Taraqi and his services, but he bought the other one, "Asia ye Javan".

He sent his errand boy to Tarqi printing house to get his magazine. I wondered how much a magazine costs for the errand boy to go all the way from "Shah Reza" Street (now Enqelab) to near "Toupkhaneh" (Imam Khomeini Square) to get a free magazine. I eagerly read whatever I could have had.

My favourite reading in *"Taraqi" Magazine* was the children's stories, which were on the first page as I opened it. In time, I'd read almost all children's stories and knew them. After this section, there were other topics in the magazine to read. "Love and the Sword" was a sequel story in the magazine that I read with interest every week. It was the story of Nader Qoli (later Nader Shah) falling in love with a girl and his struggle with his rivals. Nader Qoli's wars were also mentioned there.

The storyteller inserted whatever he wanted into the story. Sometimes, as a child, I noticed the author's lies. For example, it was written in the story that Morad hit the soldier on the back with his spear such that his backbones broke and he fell to the ground without a sound. Manuchehr Motiee wrote a crime story in it every week. Mohammad said that Lotfollah Tarqi, as a defence lawyer, provided him with criminal cases and asked him to make a story out of them.

In one of these crime stories, it was written that the criminals escaped in a Chevrolet, the latest model car. The man from the house followed them in a truck at high speed. He reached them and as he tried to stop the car, the truck ran out of fuel and stopped. Again as a child, I wondered how could a truck reach the speed of the latest Chevrolet car and even overtake it.

With all the shortcomings and pitfalls, I enjoyed reading those stories. Later, they attached a pamphlet entitled "An Iranian in the North Pole" together with Tarqi Magazine. It was also written by Manuchehr Motiee.

While in Mashhad, as a young man, Mohammad had bought a travel book which he now sold to his friend Manuchehr Motiee. For each pamphlet that was published weekly in the magazine, Mohammad received 50 Tumans. According to Mohammad, he'd taught Manuchehr Motiee how to add interesting topics to the travelogue, with his own ideas, and make it interesting and fascinating. So he added a young French girl named Ginette and an Iranian young man named Abdol Hamid to the book and let them play lovers and finally get together.

The story was so interesting that I waited impatiently all week for the next issue of the booklet to come out and enjoy reading it. Apparently, Mohammad was also captivated by these pamphlets because he himself read them in his office first before they reached me.

In the same way, Manuchehr Motiee wrote the pamphlet "The Hero of Indochina". In it, he introduced an Iranian as a hero. I also believed it and was proud that Iranians were present everywhere as heroes. It is as if in those days writers and translators did not much observe fidelity. Their books were more the product of their imaginations than the work of the original author.

My other hobby was collecting stamps. When we lived on "Rah Ahan" and I was in the second grade of elementary school, someone named Dr Ali Akbar Rezvani, a lawyer, had an office in the corridor of Mohammad's office on the beginning of Lalehzar Street. Mohammad said that he was a classmate and an old friend of Lotfollah Tarqi, and they were both from Qom. They'd come to Tehran together from Qom. Mohammad referred to him as "bad-tempered Qomi" because he had won several lawsuits in court with his cleverness and got ahead of his best friend who got nothing.

The post office had printed a series of stamps on the occasion of Soraya Esfandiari's wedding to Mohammad Reza

Shah, on 12 February 1950. Apparently, one day a friend sent two or three sets of those stamps as a gift to Dr Rezvani, and since he was not in his office, he took them to Mohammad's office to give them to him. Mohammad wasn't interested in collecting stamps, but since those series were very nice, he brought them home and gave them to me, due to his bad relationship with Dr Rezvani. I kept them until a classmate stole them from me later on. The stamps I'd lost, made me feel a strange attraction to all kinds of stamps and be diligent in collecting and putting them in an album later, as a hobby.

Amaniyeh Hill Resort, located southwest of our house, later provided some entertainment for me and my sister. Sometimes in the summer, the two of us would play rope, swing, slide, see-saw, etc. for the whole day. We gave two Tumans to the caretaker of Amaniyeh Hill in the children's playground, or we would ride a big carousel. Sometimes, I craved to live like Robinson Crusoe, whose book of the same name, by Daniel Defoe, was just published.

Reading this book gave me a great feeling of creativity. Robinson Crusoe had lived 28 lonely years on an island. One day, I cut the large branches of oleander bushes which were abundantly seen in front of our house and tied them with a rope to the top of the sycamore tree next to the entrance of our house and made a small covered hut out of them. I read books and magazines during the daytime there.

I'd just finished reading the book *Treasure Island*, by Robert Louis Stevenson. I was so impressed that one day I decided to go to the hills and valleys south of our house in search of treasure. I came out of the south gate of our garden. A couple of metres further down, there was another garden. I passed it on the right.

A small plain then appeared which led to the narrow Vojdani Street on the west, located at the foot of Amaniyeh Hill and ended at Taraz Garden, which belonged to my father's friend. I left the narrow path behind and passed by Taraz Garden towards the south. Now there were only hills and wastelands before me. It felt like I was walking in a barren, dry desert, and it reminded me of Western American movies that I often watched with my father, in which somebody was riding on horseback, or was on foot, carrying a gun, in the scorching heat of the mountains and arid deserts. There was nothing visible on my way; no birds or animals.

There were only thorn bushes growing here and there. Although I'd heard that there might be venomous snakes in those deserts, I did not think about it and passed through the desert with no fear. On a hill on my right side, my eyes caught a cave. I approached with curiosity and entered it. In the heart of the hill, there was a 2 by 3 metres room inside that looked like a den kept by the shepherds for their sheep and goats.

I saw some cigarette butts on the ground which either belonged to the thieves who'd brought the stolen goods from Elahiyeh first to that cave and smoked there to refresh themselves, before taking the stolen things to the city, or they belonged to the shepherds. From there I moved south again. I went up and down several hills and reached the top of a hill on the left side of a street. Cars were moving there. I later found out that I had actually reached the old Shemiran (Shariati) road from the hills of Abbas Abad.

As I walked, I looked at the ground to find a treasure or a sign of it. At the top of that big hill, I suddenly saw a wire that shone in the sun. Seeing it, I started digging in the ground and following the wire. Now I was sure I'd come across a treasure.

I was thrilled, but after 10 minutes of digging, I came across a tangled and thick cable. I laughed to myself. It was not a treasure, but a power or telegraph cord that I was pulling out. I stopped digging immediately because it could have been an electric wire and shocked me.

My other hobby was in our garden. In summers, after eating breakfast, I'd go to the lower garden to see what fruit had ripened. Our trees mostly consisted of cherries, purple plums, apples, pears, quince and pomegranates. Mohammad had planted tomatoes and vegetables in the plots, and in front of the entrance to the garden house, he had set aside a plot of land for strawberries. The genetically improved seeds of these strawberries were imported from California.

As a result, they bore very big fruit, the size of an adult palm, which I'd never seen anywhere before. We took them to friends and relatives as gifts. Unfortunately, the fruit grew smaller in size the next year, and in the following year, they even got as small as the indigenous strawberries.

Photo No. 12: In Elahiyeh Garden from right to left: my mother Ashraf, Dariush, my grandmother Sanam standing, my father Mohammad with my brother Kourosh in his arms, my sister Siranoush and Viki, the son of my father's friend, Jalal Farazi (autumn of 1955).

Photo No. 13: In Elahiyeh Garden next to the statue of Cleopatra, from right to left: Viki, son of Jalal Farazi, my father's friend, Ashraf, my mother, Dariush, my grandmother Sanam, little Kourosh in front of Sanam, my father Mohammad and my sister Siranoush in front of my father (autumn of 1955).

In the early days after our arrival in Elahiyeh, the streets were empty of any creature, men or animals, in the winter. No one left their home in that extreme cold, which was often below zero degrees. When we entered Fereshteh Street from Valiasr, after 50 metres on the right side, parallel to the street, there was a wasteland that went down and led to the hill of Fereshteh which turned up from the street to the top and was very dangerous in some places. In the winter, when it snowed a lot, I saw some local children sledging on it.

Photo No. 14: Graphics of sledging on the hill of Fereshteh Street.

After a while, people came from other places for sledging, so the place became almost the centre for this sport in Shemiran. I have already given enough details in the book *The Battered Generation*. Among those coming, there were some naughty chaps who harassed the people. Once I was sledging down the hill lying on my sledge, covering the last distance between the hill and the street before the stop. I suddenly heard the voice of a big, stocky young man behind me, standing on his sledge slowly coming towards me.

He wouldn't change his course not to cause an accident. Instead, he came right at me and hit his sledge on my belly. He then fell on my back with all his heavyweight. The blow was so severe that I thought my backbone broke.

My breath came out painfully. I twisted myself in pain and shouted at him and protested. The young man laughed like crazy, got up, apologised for not seeing me and went about his business.

In summer, people came to the hill of Fereshteh St for sightseeing and entertainment. Some of them drove their cars on display, or in front of each other, and tried to show the power of their Chevrolet, Pontiac, Ford or Buick cars by driving to the top of the hill, but they could only go as far as the middle and shamefully drove backwards. I just saw once, in the summer of 1957, that a Buick sped up to the top of the hill and people cheerfully applauded the driver.

Fortunately, in late March 1958, various pamphlets on criminal, historical, and social stories were published, and I began to buy and read them with my little pocket money. Reading these stories eased my loneliness. The most important thing was to read the pamphlets of "Ten Brave Men" by Shapur Arian Nejad, which transformed my life, and I waited for their publication every day. I realised I was addicted to it when I travelled to Rasht with my cousin Mansour Vahedi. From there we went to Shaft Town.

Four days later, after returning from Shaft to Rasht, I immediately rushed to the city centre and happily went to the only newspaper shop that sold the press from Tehran. From the shop window, I pointed to the pamphlet. The shop owner took it from behind the window and handed it to me. I glanced at the cover and noticed that the title was: "Azra's Kiss" by Shapur Arian Nejad. Oh, what a big mistake.

I was so fascinated by the pamphlet "Ten Brave Men" that I even saw it written on other pamphlets. With a broken heart, I sadly returned to the house of my aunt, Seyyed Fattemeh. Back in Tehran, I was able to buy the copy that I was looking for in Shemiran.

One day, I saw my mother with a young girl in her early twenties, coming to our house from the top of Fereshteh Street. When they arrived at our house, they said goodbye to each other. The girl continued on her way down Fereshteh Street and left. At home, my mother Ashraf said that the girl's name was Mastaneh, and she had helped her carry her groceries a few days ago. She also said that she lived in a house near Fereshteh Sq.

Apparently, she had recently moved to that house with her family. In the following days, I saw Niloufar, her eight or nine-year-old sister, with Siranoush, sitting by the water of Fakhr al-Dowleh, playing together. I went and sat by them. Niloufar had a beautiful and melodious voice as a child, which fascinated me when I was only 10 or 11 years old. It was then that I realised that the voice also plays a great role in attracting the opposite sex.

Days passed. One day, at the invitation of Mastaneh, Ashraf took Siranoush and me to their house to see her and Niloufar. We met their parents in the living room. After bringing tea, Mastaneh went to her father and sat on his knees. She didn't move from his knees for as long as we were there.

My mother's eyes widened in surprise. Such a big girl still considered herself a child and thought she was cute to her father. In the following days, Mastaneh explained to my mother that her father was against her marriage and always said: 'My daughter is mine. I won't give her to anyone.'

My mother was so shocked by this treatment and her upbringing that she lost contact with the family in the following weeks.

My other hobby was going to Tajrish and eating ice cream. One evening in the summer of 1958, I finished my outing in Tajrish with an ice cream and got on the Adl bus to return home. I sat on the bus on the left facing the street. Behind me sat a young couple who, from what they said, I understood that they had just been married for a few days. Apparently, their honeymoon was just coming from the city and walking around in the cool air of Shemiran and returning.

Both of them were satisfied with their journey and talked about their wishes and habits with joy and happiness. The woman said: 'I enjoy cooking at home. It's kind of fun for me. But I want my husband to wash the dishes later.'

The man said: 'There is no problem. I will do it willingly, but if you help me, we will finish them sooner together to have more time for ourselves.'

Then he continued: 'I am an early riser, but I want to sleep on Fridays like today until noon.'

The woman said: 'I also get up early, but I want you to buy me a radio so I can listen to it in the kitchen and let you sleep comfortably when I make lunch.'

They were busy talking and knowing each other. I got off at Mahmoudieh station and went home. But for many years this conversation occupied my mind. Later I came to think that in Iran, a man and a woman first get married and then get to know each other. In Europe, a man and a woman first know each other and then get married. I leave this to the reader to decide which way of marriage is better[6].

---

[6] Later, I thought that parents go to court a girl based on their own taste and opinion to find a wife for their son. A woman may be flexible and love her husband over time, even though he may not be her type, but a man does not want to marry a woman he does not like at first visit.

Photo No. 15: With the family next to the statue of Cleopatra. From right to left Kourosh; Mohammad, my father; Ashraf, my mother and Siranoush, my sister (1956).

My Reviews, Thoughts and Observations Around Our House

Mohammad bought a tricycle for Kourosh, my brother, who had just turned three.

Photo No. 16: Kourosh at the age of three (summer of 1956).

It was, however, mostly used by Siranoush or me, alone and together. Siranoush and I took the tricycle uphill to the beginning of Fereshteh Street. We rode it there. Siranoush stood on it behind me. Then we headed down the slope to our house. A tricycle with that much weight moved very fast down the hill.

God was on our side, since if a car or animal appeared before us, or my sight was blocked due to something like a fly or mosquito getting in my eye, then we were in real trouble, as I couldn't possibly break or get around that object with that high speed.

Kourosh stood at the doorway waiting for us. He looked at us as we hurried past him. In fact, he wouldn't use that tricycle at all. It was like Mohammad had bought it for us and not for him. The same tricycle caused me to ride it around the house and get acquainted with our neighbourhood and the surroundings.

Photo No. 17: Ashraf with Kourosh in the garden of Taraz, with the tricycle of Nezam, Taraz's son (summer, 1954). I used to ride around Elahiyeh on a similar tricycle later on.

Before describing the surroundings of our house, I need to briefly explain that Elahiyeh is a part of Shemiranat or

Shemiran. The question is, where the word "Shemiranat" or "Shemiran" comes from and what its origin is? There are different opinions about Shemiran. I will only make one point here that seems more logical. Shemiran comes from "Shemi" (means cool and fresh) and "ran" (means place).

It describes an area that is located at a high altitude and has a pleasant climate and fragrant flowers. This description applies to the old Shemiran. It is a region in the Alborz Mountains at higher altitudes than the city of Tehran and was once the centre of flowers, nature and beauty. Shemiranat is the plural form of Shemiran.

Elahiyeh, Fakhr al-Dowleh Street (Present "Agha Bozorgi")

Our house was located right at the intersection of Fakhr al-Dowleh (Agha Bozorgi) and Fereshteh (Morteza Fayyazi) streets. Opposite, on the north side of it, there was Fakhr al-Dowleh Street. The bare land on its east side towards Pol-e Rumi was later planted with trees of heaven and other trees, and they were irrigated from Fakhr al-Dowleh Qanat. These trees were growing fast there, and it later looked like the Amazon jungle.

Wild red and yellow flowers grew in between. Magpies, crows and sparrows had selected that place as their habitat, and their singing caressed the ear all day long. There were even raspberry bushes growing there between the trees. There was also a bare land on the west of Fakhr al-Dowleh Street where they later planted alfalfa.

Once in the following autumn, I saw a farmer patiently moving his old cow from side to side to plough the land for sowing wheat. On both sides of the street, there were walnut, aspen and sycamore trees planted. Sparrows and at times nightingales perched in abundance on their branches and sang beautifully in the trees.

About 200 metres away on Fakhr al-Dowleh Street, there was the big gate of the garden of Ali Amini, Mrs Fakhr al-Dowleh's son, on the right. He had built a house for himself on a part of his mother's land. Fruit trees in his orchard, particularly the Persian berries, attracted everybody to themselves. In the holy month of Moharram, they'd set up a large tent to accommodate almost 250 people. A low wall erected in the middle of the tent separated men from women.

Most of the time, I went there with "Nanneh Jan" (my grandmother's mother), Ashraf and Siranoush. A clergy went up to the pulpit to preach. Small tea glasses were brought in to serve the guests. On the left side of Fakhr al-Dowleh Street, almost opposite Ali Amini's house, there was a towering mud building that was said to be a large wheat mill and barn. It looked like an electric mill (it wasn't run by water).

Once there was a small fire there that went well. I only saw a small amount of smoke coming out of the building. A variety of agricultural tools could be seen around the building.

Mrs Fakhr al-Dowleh's garden was on the left side of Elahiyeh Street. There were no walls surrounding it, perhaps due to its size, even though it was private property. It was an open garden for me with no one to check the incomers. I would spend time alone there, or study with my friends and classmates in the afternoons, after school, or on vacations.

My friend "Mirza" (Houshang Khosravi), for example, used to come to our house on foot or on his bicycle. We went to Fakhr al-Dowleh's Garden together for a walk. In the summers, Mrs Fakhr al-Dowleh's gardener planted a special variety of tomatoes, each of which was the size of a palm.

Photo No. 18: In Fakhr al-Dowleh Garden, on the left side of Elahiyeh Street. From right to left: My mother, Ashraf, Nadia, the wife of Jalal Farazi, my father's friend, Viki, Jalal Farazi's son, My father, Mohammad, My brother Kourosh in front of my father, I (Dariush) and my sister Siranoush (autumn, 1957).

At the beginning of the summer, children from different places in Elahiyeh used to go to Fakhr al-Dowleh's Garden to steal berries, tomatoes, peaches and cherries. I wasn't among them and just heard about it from them. The water from the open Qanat of Fakhr al-Dowleh ran down from there, passing by our garden, to Fereshteh Street. Mrs Fakhr al-Dowleh lived in a building on the north side of the garden. It had a large iron gate.

In front of it, there was a circular area for cars to turn. The gate was always open. A football field was in front of the building where about five children played in the summer. It was said that they were orphans who were cared for and raised by Mrs Fakhr al-Dowleh. With her great wealth, people expected the number of these children to rise. Apparently, the number reached more than 20 later on.

It was almost one kilometre from there to Hesabi Junction. Along Fakhr al-Dowleh Street, after passing an endowment plot that belonged to the Endowment Office, they'd built a building on the street through which a car could pass.

Elahiyeh, Sar-e Pol-e Tajrish

I used to walk to Fakhr al-Dowleh Street (now Aqa Bozorgi) from our house on Fereshteh, most of the time. Passing by it, I'd come to Hesabi Junction and through Maqsoud Beik, I reached Tajrish. Troubles with kids of other neighbourhoods on my way had already been described in the book *The Battered Generation*, so I won't repeat it here.

I'd get out of breath to go to Tajrish on foot or on my tricycle. It was a long, upward way with lots of ups and downs. Although Tajrish was itself the centre of Shemiranat, but it was also composed of different sections. Elahiyeh and Mahmoudieh were parts of Tajrish and Shemiranat region.

On the southeast side of Tajrish Bridge, entering Shahrdari Street, there was an open and wide area called "Google" which used to be a place where cows were held. Construction workers usually stayed there every morning looking for someone to hire them. There were all kinds of fruit shops there, where my mother mostly went shopping. I used to accompany her then to help with carrying the goods. Right in front of those shops and the bazaar, there was the Adl bus station where they took the people to Tehran from Tajrish.

Sar-e Pol-e Tajrish later became a resort place of fun and entertainment for people. Following those who'd come to the region for a walk and refreshments, the hooligans of Tehran came to go to Darband or the liquor shops around. Local kids had become addicted due to their contact with the hooligans coming from Tehran. One of those kids, named Habib Alborzi, nicknamed "Habib Yakhi", who was one of Tajrish's bullies, lost his life later in 1982, due to being overdosed.

Sar-e Pol-e Tajrish was spontaneously divided into different parts for different groups, each of which had its own way, symbol and characteristic. It was the fashion centre of Tehran at that time. Those with stylish cars, brought them there to show off. Women, who'd just come back from abroad, wore their best clothes to parade in front of "Fard Cafe", on Friday mornings, to show themselves to each other.

Guys with their pretty girlfriends came there, too. Elegant people came to Fard Cafe—which belonged to "Mohammad Fard". It was considered one of the most famous and stylish cafes of that time. Or they went to "Goushvareh Talai" (Golden Earring), which belonged to "Delkash", where she herself sang at night.

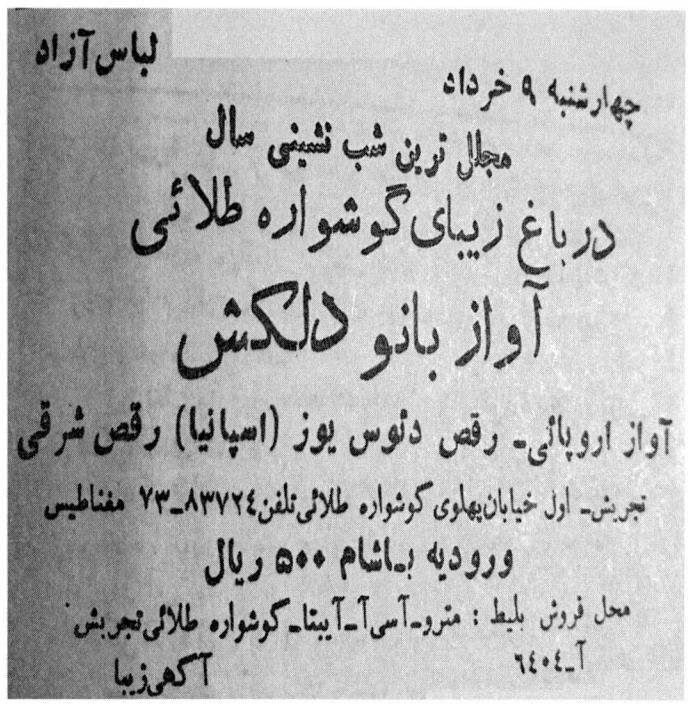

Photo No. 19: Ettela'at newspaper (1964).

On the east side of Sar-e Pol-e Tajrish, came the chador-clad women who carried a hookah and a table spread for bread and walked around and spent their time. There were "Jigaraki" (liver and heart barbecue shops) in the area, north of the Circus, favoured by the drinkers. The liquor stores were located either on Pahlavi Street or on Shahrdari Street. There were no such stores in Sar-e Pol-e Tajrish. Those who had children with them and wanted to have a healthier environment moved around the pool in the middle of the Circus.

One day, as I was coming back home, I saw a few girls, aged nine to twelve, standing by the river, chatting. I noticed a half-broken jug on a stone. I thought it was neighbourhood junk and hit it with my hand. The jug fell down on the stones by Maqsoud Beik River and broke into pieces, making a nice noise due to the crash. Suddenly, one of the girls came to it and cried: 'Why did you throw my water jug down? I wanted to get water from the spring. What can I tell my mother now?'

I noticed what wrong I'd done, but the jug was indeed worth breaking. It was so old, faded and small that one couldn't think it suitable for carrying water for a poor family. I hurried along Maqsoud Beik Street without a word. On my way, I kept thinking about how poor a family could be not to be able to afford to buy a new water jug.

Elahiyeh, Sar-e Pol-e Tajrish

From the southeast, we entered a corridor and then in a spiral to the right, we entered the "Tekiyeh" (a place for religious gatherings) and Tajrish Bazaar. There was a gate there to the south that opened to Imamzadeh Saleh. There were rooms around Imamzadeh Saleh that were the family graves of different people. To the west of it, there were small rooms for the students of the seminary in which they lived. A few hundred-year-old trees could be seen standing majestically inside the Imamzadeh.

I always enjoyed the grandeur of the tree as I passed by it, but later it seemed as if so many people had written souvenirs on it and manipulated the tree, that more than half of it had been destroyed. For a while, a cobbler set up a business in that historic tree and even slept there. On the eastern side outside Imamzadeh Saleh, small village houses with paving, ponds and small doors and windows could be seen. Local Shemiran residents rented their homes to those coming from Tehran and lived in these small rural homes instead, or set up a tent in the corner of their orchard and lived there. Otherwise, they moved out and went elsewhere.

Elahiyeh—Towards Pol-e Rumi and the Old Shemiran Road

Behind our garden house to the east, there were tall walnut and mulberry trees. As was the case with the kids at the time, I also raised silkworms on mulberry leaves and enjoyed it a lot. As a child, I wondered at the miracle of creation that turned a simple worm into a beautiful butterfly. Early in autumn when the walnuts ripened, my hands were always stained because I constantly climbed the trees to pick the walnuts and peel and break the shells to eat them. Behind our house, there was a resting place for the labourers and workers of Fereshteh Street, especially when they were filling the Hakim Hashemi River towards our house, along Fereshteh Street.

Fereshteh Street passed by our garden house and went down to Pol-e Rumi. In the year 1954, I saw Prime Minister `Ala, in a house on the left side of the street. He was having a big party and all neighbours had gathered at his entrance to watch the event. Suddenly, an expensive, black car stopped at his house and he got out and went in.

I later found out that the house belonged to him. I saw that `Ala was very short, but he showed tall in the press photos. The street went straight to Pol-e Rumi. Then it turned down to a Circus with two streets on both sides. That Circus was later called "Fereshteh Square". The lands around it all belonged to Mrs Fakhr al-Dowleh who sold them to other people through her secretary.

There was a small grocery store in the Circus. Its owner was an average-sized, kind, young man of about 23, from the province. He used to go shopping in Tajrish on his bicycle, early in the mornings or in the afternoons. Then he put the goods he'd bought in a sack, at the back of his bicycle, and took them to his shop where he sold them. Next to his grocery store, there was a bakery selling "Taftune" (a kind of bread in Iran), where we sometimes got our bread.

Since Ashraf constantly told my father that Siranoush and I were riding Kourosh's tricycle and that he kept crying for it, Mohammad finally bought me a bicycle. Now I was able to ride my own bicycle after school and on holidays and go around our area.

It was a cloudy day after the rain, and the ground was still wet. I got hold of my bike and hurried towards Pol-e Rumi. As I entered the circle, I decided to turn around and ride back home, but with my high speed on that wet ground, I slipped and hit the ground hard. A few people were standing before the grocery store. They saw me fall. One of them said: 'Ride slowly, Son!'

I was very embarrassed by what he said.

The right knee, chin and elbow of my right hand were severely injured and bleeding. The handlebars of the bicycle were tilted. I restored it to its original state, and without saying a word, I first walked home and then cycled. Ashraf had gone to Pahlavi Street to shop. I immediately cleaned the wounds.

I washed the blood, but the scars still remained. When my mother came, she blamed me a few times. Then she bandaged my hands and feet. My chin wasn't bandaged, though. She just applied a little mercurochrome on the wound.

Since then, I never saw that bike again. She'd either given it to somebody with the assistance of Hossein, our gardener or sold it at a low price. I had to use Kourosh's tricycle again for my outings.

To the right of that circle (Fereshteh Square), there was a street that led south to the hills. On either side, there were luxurious houses with large single-pane windows and a garden. They were homes to American families. Two or three times a week, I'd look at the trash behind their walls—like an antique dealer—to find their stamped envelopes.

Sometimes, there were letters in the envelopes, too. I tried to read them, but my English was not yet good enough to understand everything. Since I was walking behind their houses in the desert south of our house, I would not see many locals. After the circle, I entered Fereshteh Street, which led to Pol-e Rumi. To its right, there was the summer residence of the Turkish Embassy with its old trees; to the north was the German Embassy; and a little further south was the Russian Embassy.

Behind the German Embassy was a piece of woodland called a "slaughterhouse" because some people had once committed suicide there. As I passed through Pol-e Rumi on Kourosh's tricycle, I reached Tehran Club which was not far from the old Shemiran road. It was a gathering place for nobles, aristocrats and statesmen, such as Hossein Fardoust, who was a member. Then I drove to Tajrish. Asadi station was on the other side of the street on the right, after Pol-e Rumi.

It started up from there and ended at an area which was formerly Tajrish Endowment Cemetery. Later, the Endowment Administration handed over the lands of the cemetery and its surroundings to teachers and government employees with 99-year contracts to build their own houses there. Among those living in that area, "Jalal Al Ahmad" and "Nima Yushij" may be mentioned.

As I went further up, I came to the bus station before Dezashib. Cabs, carts and trucks also stopped there for passengers. In that area, "Jahan Hotel and Café" was seen with its prestigious gate and a large garden where celebrities like Ms Mahvash sang every night.

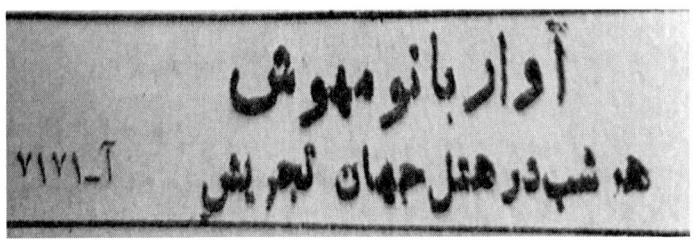

Photo No. 20: Ettela'at newspaper (Wednesday, June 13, 1956).

Nezam Agha, Mohammad's secretary, said that he worked as a waiter at the Jahan hotel and café. He also said that he served "Ashraf Pahlavi", Shah's sister and the tall, handsome young men she brought with her to spend time within a room. Nezam Aqa served them food and drink. Ashraf Pahlavi neither respected nor thanked him. The tone of her voice was authoritative.

They stayed together for a few hours and then Ashraf Pahlavi left the nightclub. Next to Cafe Jahan was a small liquor store with a garden. They served famous drinks like the Khollar vodkas of Shiraz and Minab of Isfahan, which were very strong. It was Nima Yushij's hangout, where he was said to mix his drink with Pepsi and shake his head.

Communists also went there. They drank the liquor of the Union. It was believed that Stalin's comrades drank something similar, so they followed it.

Elahiyeh—Towards the End of Pahlavi Street (Valiasr)

Sometime after we moved to Elahiyeh, in 1954, I saw that they'd started filling the dry river of "Hakim Hashemi" from the top of Fereshteh Street, which was located on the left side of the street towards Pol-e Rumi, with soil. Although the entire area belonged to Mrs Fakhr al-Dowleh, they said that she'd bought her lands from the Tajrishi people and changed the course of the river and dried up its former location to increase the price of her lands. The former course originated in the Velenjak River, which flows from the top of Fereshteh Street to the Russian Embassy in Pol-e Rumi and whence into the Maqsoud beik River.

They had already built a small bridge over the Hakim Hashemi River to go to the gardens and houses. One day, a little before two o'clock in the afternoon, as I was going to my school (Safa), I saw a black Buick car coming from the top of Fereshteh Street at a very high speed. It turned to the big gate of the house garden of the Associated Press.

The car crossed the small bridge and stood in front of the gate. Inside the car, a half-naked, blonde woman threw herself back and forth in fear and cried. A man grabbed her hand and shoulder and tried to calm her down. It appeared that the woman's shirt had been torn or taken out due to the crash in the car. Again, it appeared that a foreign woman had been abducted from outside and forcibly taken to that house garden to be raped. The driver was in a hurry.

When the gardener heard the horn he opened the door. The driver rushed in so speedily that the car's wheels sounded in place as he drove to the house at the end of the garden. I was still a child. I could not do anything for that woman, so I continued on my way. Later, remembering this memory hurt me a lot.

As the river filled, an empty space was created which made Fereshteh Street slightly larger in width.

The land at the corner of Fakhr al-Dowleh and Fereshteh streets was barren and full of thorny bushes. It belonged to a gentleman named "Bina" who later built a house there and moved in with his family. About 50 metres up Fereshteh Street, he built another one-story house and rented it to an English couple named Linda and Martin with two children. Between the two houses, there was a barren land full of thorny bushes. As Mohammad later said, the rent for their house at that time was 1,300 Tumans.

In the beginning, my mother, Ashraf, wasn't very much in touch with Martin's wife, Linda, because she didn't know her language. Their kind, Assyrian maid, Mehri, who was around 20, often visited us. Entering their house, there was an open space where Martin parked his car. It led to the entrance of the building. Along the wall of the house to the south, about 3 metres away from the entrance door, they had made a small room for the servant.

It was about 2 metres above the ground level, and they entered it by climbing a few steps. Mehri lived in that room.

When Ashraf wanted to see her, she called her from the window outside. Then Mehri opened the window above and talked to my mother.

Behind their house on the west side, there was a wasteland. The English family dumped their garbage there. I constantly checked it to see if I could find the stamps of their discarded envelopes there. Towards Christmas, they received many letters from England with beautiful Christmas stamps. The stamps were very small and had pictures of a child on them in various shapes.

I got all the Christmas stamps from 1955 to 1956. Then I thought it was not pleasant for me to look in people's trash to find stamps, so I left it to my classmates to do it, and from then on, I bought the stamps from them. The garbage was collected by the municipality once a week.

Entering Pahlavi Street on the right, next, there was Amir Teimur Street.[7]

A little further down, we got to the narrow and long street of "Kazemi" (now Takhti).[8]

Although the street was narrow and winding, there were great people living there. Here I will only briefly mention a few famous families. When we entered Kazemi Street (present-day Takhti), in front of the entrance of Bagh-e Ferdos High School,[9] from Ez al-Dowleh Square (now Takhti Square), ending at Fereshteh Street, the first large garden on the right belonged to Dr Gholam Reza Rashid Yasemi, a Tehran University professor. On the left, there was Nouri

---

[7] That street was later called Bosnia and Herzegovina.

[8] Previously, that street was called Rashid Yasemi.

[9] It was later named "Shapur of Tajrish" and then "Jalal Al-Ahmad".

Esfandiari's garden, which was known as Esfandiari Garden. To its left, the garden of Dr Parviz Kazemi could be seen, facing the stylish house of "Hassan Pirayesh".[10]

In that street, there were other houses such as the house of "Colonel Mehdi Khaza'i".[11] Some other personalities living there were "Gholam Reza Takhti", "Haji Laleh".[12]

"Commander Mohtashami", the Commander of the Khorasan Army under Reza Shah, "Ruhollah Khaleghi", a composer, and finally, at the end of Kazemi that meets Fereshteh, there was the house of the Commander of the Imperial Guard, "Nematollah Nasiri", who later went to Niavaran and became the head of the Security Organisation.

At that time, people loved Gholam Reza Takhti and hated Dr Kazemi because he was related to the court. He had long upset the residents of the street saying that he intended to name the street after himself. For this reason, they gave each other the name of Takhti Alley when giving the address,

---

[10] He had the well-known "clothing shop Pirayesh" which was between "Toupkhaneh" and the Iran Cinema on the right side towards Istanbul crossroads.

[11] He later became the head of Tehran's traffic police and was later executed. He was a classmate of Mohammad Reza Shah and Hossein Fardoust in the military school, for 6 years. The school was an elementary school, not a high school. During the reign of Reza Shah, high-ranking army officials had set up that school for their children only. Mohammad Reza Shah also studied there until the fifth grade and then he went directly to Switzerland. There was another military school that they attended from the tenth grade on and later from the eleventh grade. and his brothers.

[12] He was the chairman of the Bank of Tehran and one of its founders. He was short and had a big belly.

although the exact name of the street had not yet been determined. Finally, the residents of the street named it "Rashid Yasemi" because he used to live there in his large garden, before moving to Niavaran. Besides, he was a university professor and the name suited him more.

Later, however, Dr Parviz Kazemi decided to name the street after his daughter "Jaleh", instead of "Rashid Yasemi". A lawsuit was filed. The fight was going on. At night, you would see that the tile with the name "Jaleh" had been removed and "Rashid Yasemi" was replaced. The next morning, on my way to school, I'd see that it was changed again.

For a while, changing the name of Kazemi Street to "Rashid Yasemi" on the right side of the street and then "Rashid Yasemi" to "Jaleh" caught my attention, on my way to school. I was confused by this change of letters, like other neighbours and passers-by. Finally, Dr Parviz Kazemi had the upper hand and "Jaleh" remained, due to his powerful position.

In this way, peace and tranquillity returned to that street. Residents then widened the street to improve it. Later, because the late Gholam Reza Takhti, the famous ring athlete, had a house on Jaleh Street and the locals wanted the street to be named after him, they named it "Takhti".

There were barren lands facing the exit of Takhti Street in Fereshteh. In the same area to the right, there was a large plot of land that ran into the hills of Fereshteh Street. This land belonged to an old man who was a native of Tajrish. A colonel saw the land unoccupied and built a wall around it to register it in his name. A fight broke out between the colonel and the old man.

The sad old man destroyed the walls built on his land. He said that the colonel of the country had abused his position and seized his land by force. The colonel made plans and called the old man. He told him: 'Let's sit down together and solve our problems. I'll buy your land and will satisfy you. Leave it to me.'

The old man went to the colonel's house. The colonel beat him well in his house with some soldiers who had been assigned, claiming that "you came and raped my wife". They even imprisoned the old man. Neighbours, friends and acquaintances of the old man knew that the colonel had neither bought the land nor did he have any documents for it. Undocumented lands usually went to the natives, not to a colonel who came from the city and said, 'I own this place.'

The people helped the old man and took back the land from the colonel. The old man dedicated the land to the mosque after this incident. Later, at the beginning of Fereshteh Street, a mosque called "Fereshteh Mosque" was built, the founder and builder of which was "Haj Kazem Mohseni".

Elahiyeh, from Fereshteh Street (Morteza Fayyazi) along Pahlavi Road (Valiasr)

I started walking towards Pahlavi Street from home, one Friday. As I entered Pahlavi Street, right on the left-hand side, there was a restaurant named "Chelokababi ye Tabriz no" which belonged to a fat-bellied Haji. Next to it, there was a laundry shop where my mother took Mohammad's clothes at his request. Then there was the "Arbab Jamshid" grocery store. "Arbab Jamshid" was an army man who had come to Tehran from Yazd with his brother, Yaqub.

He'd opened a grocery store in Mahmoudieh with his wife and they ran it together. They were a Zoroastrian couple. Yaqub also started his snack bar known as "Khoshnoud" between Mahmoudieh and the next station, Homayouni. He was the representative of the Zoroastrians of Tehran. Homayouni station was named after Colonel Homayouni.

He lived in a stylish, two-storey house on the right-hand side of Tehran-Tajrish road, located on a side street from Pahlavi Street. In the past, Homayouni station was known as "Istgah-e Cheraq-e Akhar" (the last lamp station).

Arbab Jamshid was known as "Arbab" to us. It was a tradition to call the Zoroastrians "Arbab", the Armenians "Monsieur" and the Indians "Sahib". Ashraf usually bought her groceries from Arbab Jamshid on credit. Mohammad sometimes forced Ashraf to go and borrow two Tumans from Arbab to pay for his trip to the city by bus or taxi. She'd buy a small sack of rice, a 5 kg tin container of cooking oil and other groceries from Arbab and asked him to record all that in his notebook to be paid at the end of the month.

But, at times, she couldn't even pay it at the end of the month and asked him to leave it for the next month. Arbab Jamshid wouldn't mind it and got along friendly with his customers. There weren't many families living in that area, therefore, the shopkeepers had to get along with this limited number of customers. Poor Ashraf had to feed us somehow because Mohammad had money one day and went without the next month.

Arbab Jamshid's family loved Ashraf, and so did she. She was very kind to them. When she heard that Arbab's wife was pregnant and was going to have a baby soon, she gave her Kourosh's cradle so she wouldn't need to pay for a new one. Ashraf didn't need it at that time, but when my sister, Hourvash, was born, she got the cradle back because she couldn't afford a new one.

As they were working on foot all day long, Arbab Jamshid and his wife had pain in their legs. Mohammad suggested they cover the floor with wooden slats so they wouldn't get rheumatism from the dampness of the floor. They immediately took his advice and did it. Arbab Jamshid was run over by a car one day as he was crossing the street, and he died. Ashraf was very sad and mournful for a while because of this event. They were a kind and quiet Zoroastrian couple and were very friendly to everyone.

Right after Arbab Jamshid's grocery store, there was Mohammad Yekta's confectionery shop. He was previously the Chef of the Fard café in Tajrish. His confectionery business wasn't profitable, though, as Tehranis mostly came to our area in summertime for its cool weather. They'd return to their homes in Tehran late in August, and Elahiyeh wasn't then a resort any more.

As a result, he didn't have many customers. With his experience at Fard Café, Mohammad Yekta decided to change his shop to a snack bar where he sold sandwiches and ice cream. He served a variety of fruit juice there, as well as fruit ice cream and sandwiches.

Now the Villa ice cream shop at Tajrish sq. had to close down as everybody came to Yekta. I hardly dropped by there during the day, but sometimes Siranoush and I bought sour cherry or lemon ice cream from him. The price for a simple ice cream was four Rials then. We'd eat them with pleasure on our way back home.

This was our fun day to walk on the street and eat something on our way. When coming back home from the city at night, in his jeep, with Mohammad, he'd stop at Yekta snack bar to have an apple or quince juice there together. The café was empty and I often asked myself how they could run their business with such an empty shop. Mohammad talked with the shop owner and the workers there very warmly and gave them tips because they respected us very much every time we went there.

I later heard that Yekta snack bar was running a good business. People parked on the street close to the shop and ate his delicious sandwiches and drank his fruit juice. His snack bar became one of the best in Shemiranat. His Salad Olivier was very famous. Its good business may have been due to the fact that new people have moved and settled down in that area and populated Mahmoudieh.

There was an enclosed place next to Mohammad Yekta's snack bar with fallen bricks. Then there was a wasteland on the east of which Amaniyeh Hill was located. Pahlavi Street had a steep slope at the foot of Amanieh Hill to Fereshteh Street. Trucks and buses had a hard time there moving up.[13]

---

[13] Esfandiar Hassel Nejad, who was connected to the Court through Ms Panahi, drove from the Pahlavi intersection to Bagh-e Ferdos one evening, in seven minutes. He did it to show off the power of his car, but this was a sign that there wasn't much traffic on that road at that time, in the modern sense.

Amanieh Hill

There were three hills there, of which the highest one on the south was later called Amanieh Hill. In the beginning, Amanieh Hill was a conical hill like Damavand and Ararat mountains. The front part of it, facing Pahlavi Street, was turned into a ski resort.

Those with the necessary equipment went there to ski. It was a nice hill where Mohammad Reza Shah also used to go skiing. Its present location can now be described as limited to Ayatollah Modarres highway on the north and east, Valiasr on the west and close to Khakzad and Turaj on the south.

All along the south of Amanieh Hill was a barren land. There was no local water available there yet. Colonel Amani bought that hill and its surroundings and thus they named it Amanieh after him.[14]

After levelling the tip of Amaniyeh Hill, there came the water problem. It was solved by bringing water from the Moshiri garden in Velenjak to Amanieh Hill, all through the

---

[14] The letter "H" at the end of the word "Amaniyeh" indicates possession in Persian grammar. Some claim on the internet that Colonel Amani's surname was originally "Amanpour", and that this surname became common in Reza Shah's Era.

efforts of Colonel Amani who also carried out the water plumbing in the Shemiran region. Before transferring water to Amaniyeh, they had asked Mahmoud Keshtkar to visit the Moshiri garden. He'd then said that the water there wouldn't last for long. It was indeed as he said because if a deep well is dug vertically, it gets close to the source of the water, and it is also fed from its surroundings, but a well dug in the mountain which reaches water might soon be finished one day, due to the small source of water available there.

As some might think, Colonel Amani hadn't dug the well in the Velenjak area. He had, in fact, done it horizontally in the middle of the mountain and hit an immense source of water which he then piped to the top of Amaniyeh Hill through cast iron pipes.[15]

Colonel Amani was the first one to draw the water pipe from Velenjak to Amaniyeh, and by so doing, he brought prosperity to Amaniyeh and its surrounding orchards and houses, especially to the area behind it to the east. Then he started a restaurant and a pool with large fountains and a nice place for healthy entertainment for children and adults to enjoy spending their time at. He himself lived in that place. Swings, see-saws, a carousel and slides, as well as a basketball ground were some of the play equipment there. The caretaker of Amaniyeh was a tall young man with dark skin

---

[15] Amaniyeh Hill's water decreased later on. Some people said that it was due to the exhausted water reservoir in the mountain. However, others believed that the water piped from Velenjak was sold to various houses on the way and used there, and this caused a shortage for Amaniyeh.

who was called "Mohammad Amaniyeh", but he must originally have had a different surname himself.

Photo No. 21: Graphics of Amaniyeh Hill.

Pahlavi Street (now Valiasr) was widened in the year 1955. This was the first step in the development of that area. Following the supply of water and the building of Amaniyeh Street, which continued to the top of the hill in a spiral way, people started building 11–14 stylish and modern houses around that area. These houses were mostly leased to the Americans, particularly to American advisors, and the intellectual Iranians who'd studied in the United States.

Then more constructions followed, and as you entered Amaniyeh Street from Pahlavi Rd., you'd see nice and modern houses going around and reaching to the top of Amaniyeh Hill. I walked a few times from Pahlavi Road to the top of the hill, and by the time I got there, I was panting hard and felt short of breath. I could see the city of Tehran there, down at my feet.

A police station was set up there at the very beginning of Amaniyeh Street towards the left hill. This was due to the frequent robberies which had taken place in that area and for the safety of the Americans and the other residents. It was the Mahmoudieh branch of the Tajrish police station. The surrounding area of Amaniyeh was kind of suspicious. People thought crimes and felonies took place there.

They said that the Security Organisation personnel lived in that area, but according to the census of the year 1959, it was known that the majority of its residents were the followers of the Baha'i faith for unknown reasons. In the census form, they'd written "Muslim, Christian, Jewish, etc." in front of the religion. Baha'i was included in "etc." Some Baha'is said: 'I will only answer your question if you write Baha'i there.'

One had to be brave enough to do this because at that time, "Mohammad Taqi Falsafi", a well-known clergyman, was campaigning actively against the Baha'is. For two or three years before that time, Falsafi criticised the Baha'is severely at one o'clock in the afternoon, on the radio. Muslims had started a secret committee called "Anjoman Hojatieh Mahdavieh" against the Baha'is. This was conducted by a man called "Sheikh Mahmoud Halabi" who aimed at destroying the Baha'i faith.[16]

---

[16] Taking the census was the right thing to do; they wanted to know the population of Elahiyeh and see if they needed a school or a high school, etc. Or if it was a lower-class area to set up a small clinic

Amaniyeh Hill, originally called "Amaniyeh Park", was very active in the beginning with its advertisement put everywhere.[17]

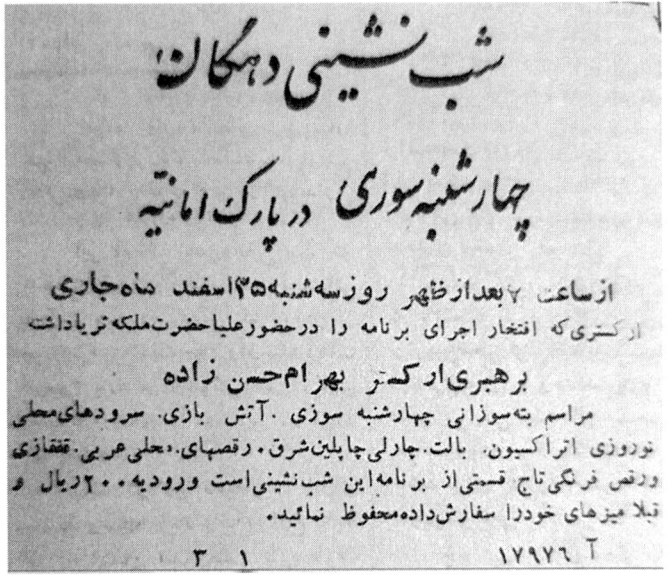

Photo No. 22: Ettela`at Newspaper advertisement for Amaniyeh Hill (Tuesday, 23 February 1954).

---

there. They provided all the data to the Budget and Planning Organisation to work on. They started with good intentions, but after some time a new team with different opinions replaced them and things changed.

[17] Amaniyeh; People of good taste, interested in nature, fine music and good meals never forget Amaniyeh Park. Amaniyeh Park is welcoming you with excellent music." Ettela'at Newspaper, Monday, October. 19, 1953.

Late-night parties were arranged there during the summers. Occasionally, good-natured young locals celebrated on Amaniyeh Hill and sold tickets to young people and the Americans. They emptied the water in its pool and turned it into a dancing stage. That was when "Rock and Roll" had become fashionable. During nights, we could hear the sound of the fast foreign music and the loud laughter of the guests from our garden house behind Amaniyeh Hill.

People of Tehran were very thirsty for these programmes, but why wouldn't they participate in Amaniyeh Hill celebrations and went to the clumsy parties of the municipality at "Shah Reza-Pahlavi intersection" (now Enqelab-Valiasr) instead, which was always crowded? It was because people didn't have their own car to drive to Amaniyeh. It was hard for them to go to Amaniyeh by Adl bus and walk to the top of the hill to drink a glass and have fun.

On the other side of Pahlavi Street, just a few steps further down from Fereshteh Street, there was a Sangak (a kind of Iranian bread) bakery. We all bought our bread from that shop. At times, you'd find a roasted cockroach in the bread, too. The bakery also had a delivery man who carried the bread on a cart and took it to people's homes.

We sometimes got our bread like that from the bakery. It wasn't fresh, though, so people sent their gardeners to buy the bread from the shop. Sometimes when I bought our bread myself, I noticed that they also sold toast bread there. They said that it was for their diabetic customers.

One day, when Mohammad and I were visiting Lotfollah Taraqi, we saw some toast bread among others there, as he was having his breakfast. Mohammad told me it was because Taraqi was diabetic.

The Azizi grocery store was next to the bakery. It was more of a dairy shop than a grocery store. The shop owner's son, Massoud Azizi, was my classmate at Safa School, but I rarely saw him in that shop. We sometimes went there for shopping, but we mostly went to Arbab Jamshid's. A coffee house and a blacksmith shop were opened between the Sangak bakery and Azizi grocery store, later on.

Lotfollah Taraqi's house was located next to the Azizi grocery store. He was the editor of "Taraqi" and "Asia ye Javan" Magazines. The green stones of the wall of his house gave it a special beauty. A few steps away, one reached the large gate of the house where his car entered. He had a gardener, a driver and a servant at his house.

His skilful gardener had planted the best variety of flowers in his house. As we entered, walking up, we passed the row of colourful flowers and trees leading to the building located to the north and to the right of the entrance of the house. Next to his building, there was a barren land which continued to the "Vanak" and "Abshar" intersection.

Following the details mentioned above, I see it as a good time to start talking about my own five years living at Elahiyeh.

Second Part
Rain and Great Luck to Valiollah, Our Gardener

My mother, Ashraf, arranged Valiollah's room on the west side of the corridor. She laid a mat, a blanket and a pillow there for him to rest. It gradually got darker a little earlier in the evenings. Autumn rain was falling nonstop, and we'd adapted ourselves to the weather.

Ashraf slowly took out our autumn and winter clothes from the closets to wear. It was the first year of our stay in Elahiyeh. We didn't have much experience living outside the city and in that barren valley.

It was heavily raining one night. We were all idle at home looking at the rain through the window before we went to sleep after dinner. In the middle of the night, we suddenly heard a scary sound. We all came out of the rooms to see what had happened. Ashraf soon found the reason for that terrible noise.

Immediately, she opened the door of Valiollah's room. At once, she saw that heavy plaster straw of the ceiling had fallen on the southwest corner of the room and water was dripping from the ceiling. Valiollah was in such deep sleep that he hadn't even noticed the fall. Ashraf woke him up immediately. Mohammad also left his room and checked the ceiling. He sadly said: 'These dishonest builders have cheated us. They didn't do a proper job.'

Ashraf was very scared. She kept saying: 'God had mercy on Valiollah. If the roof had fallen on his side, he would have been crushed under it.'

The next day, Mohammad called the builder who had tricked him and told him what had happened the night before. The builder came with a few workers the same afternoon and they repaired the whole roof to prevent future accidents. Then they repaired Valiollah's room to its former state and left. Valiollah was able to sleep in peace in that room from then on.

In the evenings, Ashraf would throw a blanket on the northwest side of the hall, and we sat together. Valiollah would also join our small gathering with Ashraf, Nanneh Jan, Siranoush, Kourosh and I. Ashraf would place the teapot next to the stove she'd put on the blanket. We drank tea and talked about everything. One night, Nanneh Jan talked about her memories of the First World War and its aftermath when hungry Russian soldiers rushed to Rasht.

They went from house to house and looted people's valuable belongings. She said that right after Ashraf's mother was born, and while she was recovering at home, the Russians, four or five of them, came to their house after inspecting nearby houses. The first thing they did was going to Nanneh Jan's room. They took the gold and silver objects she had hidden under her pillow. She begged them to leave some for her, but those men, who spoke a little Persian and seemed to be coming from Russian Azerbaijan, took everyone with them, regardless of her request.

It would not matter if the Tsarist Russians were on the side of Moscow or Azerbaijan (Soviet). In any case, they were hungry soldiers looking for spoils of war. After the words of Nanneh Jan, Valiollah, who was over 40 years old and had enough life experience, started palm reading for Ashraf and Nanneh Jan. His words were good and hopeful.

In the meantime, Mohammad arrived. Ashraf told him that Valiollah could read palms and predict one's future. Mohammad told her his predictions might be useful for his friends and clients and give them good results, but for the person himself, it will bring nothing but misery. He continued: 'Experience shows that the fortune teller himself is not and will not be a happy person.'

Valiollah heard everything but said nothing. He drank his tea and went to his room. Early in winter, he returned to his province because his wife and children needed him in that cold weather.

We spent all that hard winter alone with Nanneh Jan and my sister and brother. There was no city traffic there to warm up the air.

Fighting over Water— Mohammad Our New Gardener

Springtime arrived, and Mohammad looked for a new gardener to help him with planting flowers and trees in the garden. One day, Mohammad entered the house with a 26-year-old young man from Sabzevar, who was also named Mohammad. He told us that Mohammad was our gardener from then on. He gave him the room on the west side of the hall which belonged to Valiollah before.

Ashraf spread his beddings there and provided him with all the necessities of life such as pots, pans and plates. He himself had a primus cooker (a kind of kerosene cooker without the wick) on which he cooked for himself. Ashraf put an oil heater in his room, too, because he would get cold under his blanket at night.

Once when Ashraf was going to the restroom at night, she heard a loud snoring sound from Mohammad, in the gardener's room. Forgetting what she'd come out for, she rushed to his room and opened the door. There she noticed the smell of oil and the heat filling the room, while Mohammad was being suffocated from lack of oxygen. Ashraf immediately cried and called my father. Then she opened the window and turned off the oil heater, which was running at a very high flame.

My father immediately took Mohammad, the gardener, out of the room, who was almost unconscious. He massaged his shoulders and slapped him on the face a few times to make him come to his senses. Then he told him to take a few deep breaths in the cold outside. Apparently, the gardener had felt cold early at night and raised the flame of the oil heater too high. As a result, the oil could not burn as much at the same time as the flame. Therefore, the air got polluted and drifted him into a mild unconsciousness.

Had it not been for Ashraf's going to the restroom by accident, we would have definitely encountered the cold body of Mohammad, the gardener, the following morning. He stayed with us all spring with two months of summer. Towards sunset, he used to make himself broth or kebab every day. The smell of his delicious broth and grilled kebab had driven us crazy. Siranoush and I gathered around him to see how he prepared food.

He mixed the minced meat well with the onion and egg yolk and beat it in a bowl with his fist for a while. Then he'd skewer and grill the meat. Ashraf did not get enough money from Mohammad for our food, so she couldn't cook delicious meals for us. Our food was mainly "Baqala Qatuq", "Mirza Qasemi" or tomato omelette with eggs. We later brought the eggplant and tomatoes from our own garden.

Several times, Mohammad invited us children to a barbecue with bread, even though he did not have enough money, which we ate with great pleasure. But then we were embarrassed to gather around him while cooking his meal. Earlier that summer, Mohammad said he missed his wife and young child. So my father allowed him to bring his family to live with him, too. His wife was a kind woman and helped Ashraf with housekeeping. Mohammad gave them more money for that from then on.

As usual, we got water from Amaniyeh Hill, and it was dumped into our house once a week. Mohammad paid for the water in advance. The water irrigated the trees in the lower garden before it was stored in the reservoir, but that water would barely meet our weekly needs. To do everything easily, we had to get water twice, but Mohammad did not always have the money to pay for it.

For this reason, when Fakhr al-Dowleh water passed by our house on Fereshteh Street, either I or Mohammad, the gardener, supplied some of it to irrigate the lower garden. One day, when the water share of other gardens was passing from Amaniyeh by our house, I found out that the gardener had made a little brook to divert it to our garden. He might have been doing this wrong to please my father.

There was a tall, slender young man of about 26 years old, living on top of Amaniyeh Hill. His name was Hossein Aqa. At times, he watched the water supply flowing to other gardens from above. One day he saw that Mohammad, the gardener, went to the mainstream with his shovel and opened a side stream for us where water was flowing into someone else's garden. He shouted from up there: 'What are you doing there? Why are you diverting other people's water?'

He kept repeating his words, but the gardener wouldn't pay any attention to what he said and kept on doing it. The water watch saw that Mohammad wouldn't listen to what he was saying. So he angrily descended the Amaniyeh Hill by sliding down the steep slope of the hill. As he descended, he kept shouting to Mohammad to stop the flow of water from the mainstream to our garden. However, the gardener wouldn't react to his outrage. Outside, Ashraf, the gardener's wife and her child, Siranoush and I were standing together.

Hossein Aqa reached the back of the south side of our house like a wild animal and got into a fight with Mohammad, the gardener. He knocked him to the ground with a few blows and threw himself on him. The weak body of Mohammad did not have the strength to stand up to Hossein, a well-trained and well-fed young man. We suddenly saw that he was being suffocated under the arms and legs of Hossein Aqa. Mohammad's wife shouted at the sight and then cried.

Her child was crying, too. Shocked by what was going on, Ashraf shouted at Hossein Aqa, saying: 'What are you doing to our gardener, you monster? Leave him alone!'

I was upset with this unequal fight, but I wasn't strong enough to separate them from each other and discipline Hossein Aqa.

Mohammad was trying to free himself from Hossein Aqa's grasp in dust, in that hot summer. Eventually, as a result of our shouts, he stopped beating him and left Mohammad with a bleeding nose and a broken head, warning him not to do it again or he'd be badly punished.

I was more upset because of the wife and child of Mohammad, who saw him being beaten by the monster Hossein and could not help him. This humiliation and shame of being beaten in front of his wife and child must not have been very pleasant for Mohammad, the gardener, either because, a week later, he settled his account with my father, took his wife and child's hand and left our house. After a while, Mohammad hired another gardener, also with the same name, Hossein.

Photo No. 23: Dariush at the age of 10 in the garden of Fereshteh Street in Elahiyeh, in the summer of 1954 (taken from the book *The Battered Generation*).

The Story of the Worker Digging a Well in Elahiyeh

In this chaotic state of water shortage, one day a well-digger came. He said to Mohammad: 'Why do you buy water? I can dig a well for you to drink water and irrigate your garden and get rid of the water problem forever.'

Mohammad answered: 'No, it's not possible. They say there's no water in this area. The Qanat water comes from somewhere out of our garden.' Then he pointed to the other side of the house where water could exist. However, the well-digger didn't give up. He continued: 'I guarantee that in less than 50 metres we'll reach the water.'

He talked and praised his work so much that Mohammad finally agreed. The well-digger started his work the next day. He brought with him someone to help him. They kept working for 10 days but in vain. By the end of the second week, he came to Mohammad and told him that he had to pay his worker and needed money.

Mohammad told him: 'We stipulated that I would give you money when the well reached the water. What money do you want from me?'

The well-digger didn't give up and insisted on taking the money. They started an argument and got into a fight. Ashraf and Ms Parvaneh, our tenant, were present there. They started shouting: 'Get separated! Let go of each other!'

Our gardener Hossein Aqa, who had a large body, did not say anything. He just stood there and watched the fight, because Mohammad was his master.

As a result of fighting and jumping on each other, suddenly both men fell to the ground. Mohammad placed himself on the well-digger's chest and began to squeeze his throat. The well-digger's face was turning black. My mother and our tenant, Parvaneh, were now screaming in worry. They looked at Hossein Aqa and shouted at him to separate them.

He eventually separated Mohammad from the well-digger who got up like a beaten dog, and crying, he picked up his belongings and went away. Later, Hossein Aqa told me: 'That day, I wanted to hit him in the head with a shovel out of anger, because your father did not want to pay the well-digger his wage.'

I had nothing to say to him. All I knew was that there was something wrong with what the well-digger did.

Photo No. 24: Ashraf and Mohammad (author's mother and father) in the upper garden, in front of the building (summer of 1954).

Planning Our Lunch
by Mohammad

One day after Mohammad came home, he told Ashraf: 'I'm tired of eating Nanneh Jan's Baqala Qatuq and nasty foods. I want to eat something delicious.'

Ashraf stood before him and said: 'Give me more money to cook you the best meals. Just be thankful for what you eat without much money paid for it.'

Mohammad went to his room and started planning on a piece of paper. A quarter of an hour later, he came out of the room with a piece of paper and stuck it to the wall of our living room. He asked for a different meal every day of the week. Calf's brain with chips on Saturday, or eggplant stew. Qormeh Sabzi (a kind of Persian stew cooked with meat and vegetables) on Sunday, Cutlet and chips, or lamb's liver, heart and kidney on Monday.

For Tuesday, he asked for kebab. Calf's tongue for Wednesday, rice cooked with veggies and fish for Thursday and sirloin steak or barberry pilaf with chicken for Friday. He also wanted to have a kind of soup with every meal as well as a seasonal salad. He paid for all this in advance for a week, so Ashraf would easily see to them.

Ashraf was thrilled by this generosity. She'd start early in the morning to go all that way from Elahiyeh to Pahlavi Street to buy the ingredients from Arbab Jamshid's grocery store. Most of the time, she went to the Tajrish market by bus to buy fruits and vegetables there. Poor Ashraf carried the heavy load alone and with the help of Nanneh Jan, they prepared the food that Mohammad wanted.

Mohammad came home on time and ate his own lunch. This program lasted for two or three weeks until Mohammad's money ran out. He no longer paid a week in advance but paid daily. Then the daily payment was stopped due to the father's financial problems. Ashraf had to fill our stomachs again with cheap food or buy on credit from Arbab Jamshid.

A Fake Couple Moving to Our House

One late summer day, a beautiful young woman about 23 or 24 years old named Parvaneh, knocked on our garden house door and asked for the owner of the house. My father wasn't at home, so my mother talked to her. She told my mother that she was looking for a vacant room in our area to live with her husband, who was a taxi driver in the city. She was a sweet-talking, pretty woman. Ashraf liked her at once and said: 'Yes, we have an empty room. I'll talk about it with my husband tonight and shall let you know tomorrow. You can also come and talk to him yourself tonight after nine.'

The room intended by Ashraf was actually our living room where we also slept. My mother was getting sick of living in solitude in that area and thought that women could make her good company.

Talking to Mohammad at night, we decided to rent that room on the east side to that couple and live ourselves in the hall and go to Ashraf and Mohammad's room for sleep. Two days later, the couple moved into our building. They did not have much furniture; just a mattress and a quilt with a few kitchen utensils. Her husband, Manuchehr Khan, was a polite, well-dressed and slender man, about 29 or 30 years old, and he had a new, stylish English Maurice Minor car.

It looked like he had just got it from the company. Mohammad had taken his jeep to a mechanic in the city once, and we had no car the next morning. Manuchehr Khan gave us a ride to Mohammad's office. His car had soft and comfortable seats and was warm.

The couple had been staying in our house for two weeks now, and my mother had gotten used to them. She was in touch with Parvaneh, who was a kind and warm woman with a nice personality, the whole day. They went shopping together. They cooked together. And they spent their leisure time in the hall chatting until their husbands returned home from work. They had now become two inseparable friends.

One Friday, a woman knocked on our door. She said she wanted to see Manuchehr Khan whom she guessed was living in our house. Ashraf said: 'Yes, such a gentleman lives here.'

Then she led her to Manuchehr and Parvaneh's room. Nanneh Jan, my mother and us were in the hall. Mohammad was working with trees and flowers in the garden. Suddenly, we heard the sound of an object falling to the ground from Parvaneh's room. After about a minute, Parvaneh rushed out of her room.

She went to my mother and told her: 'Ashraf Khanum, something has happened. I have to go. I wish you good health. Take care of yourself and the children. I am very happy to have met you.'

Then she left us in a hurry. We were all surprised. What had happened? After a few moments, the woman who'd asked us about Manuchehr Khan showed up. Her name was Pouran. She went to my mother and apologised to her. She said: 'The girl who just left your house is my sister. She is a naughty girl and has close relations with my husband. My husband and I are married for two years. My sister always wanted to attract him to herself.'

We listened to her in surprise. Ashraf was silent and didn't say a word. Mohammad kept silent, too. The formal wife had found her husband and was living with him. My father saw no reason for intervention.

Days passed. One day, while talking, my mother asked Pouran: 'What was the sound of that object falling when you entered the room?'

When I entered the room. I saw my bad sister next to my husband. I lost control. I started hitting her and pulling her hair.

I said: 'What are you whore doing with my husband! I got into a fight with her. We both fell to the ground. My husband separated us. He covered my mouth so that you could not hear my shouting.'

Days later, a friendly relationship developed between Ashraf and Pouran. The two women sat together and talked about everything. Now they'd become close friends. A couple was also added to our family, and with Nanneh Jan and Hossein Aqa, the gardener, we wouldn't feel lonely in the evenings any more. But, over time, there came a separation between Ashraf and Pouran.

My mother stopped her contact with Pouran for a few days. One night after my father came back home from work, she told him: 'Pouran is not a good woman. She constantly talks behind her own family and attributes bad things to them. She is also very curious about our married life. I can't bear her in our house any more. Let her go!'

Mohammad called Pouran and Manuchehr Khan the next day and told them that a guest would arrive from Rasht in the coming days and that he needed their room for him. He asked them to evacuate the room soon. Pouran tried hard to convince Mohammad to let them stay there for a few more weeks, but Mohammad refused.

The day Pouran and Manuchehr Khan put their belongings in the car and wanted to leave, Pouran came to our building again and said goodbye to us. When going to Mohammad, she said: 'Mr Pourkian, I have a few private words with you.'

Mohammad left the building with her. They both walked slowly towards the garden entrance. Ashraf Khanum, the wife of Esmail Hozuri, my mother's cousin, was our guest then. She was picking green beans from the vine from the patch next to the wall for our lunch that day.

At that moment, she heard Pouran telling Mohammad: 'Mr Pourkian! You've got to keep a close watch on your wife. She is interested in Hossein Aqa, your gardener. She told me a few times about her love for him and said many good things about him to me.'

At this, Mohammad stood firm in his place. He said: 'Ma'am, what are you talking about? My wife has a 14-year-old son at home. She has two other children. There is a baby in her womb. Shame on you for slandering my wife.'

My mother was two months pregnant with Hourvash. Pouran did not say another word. She lowered her head and left. Mohammad turned to us inside the building and said to my mother without going into details: 'We got rid of this nasty woman.'

The Danger of Me Drowning in Amanieh Pool

One summer day, Turan, my aunt, came to see us. Siranoush, Kourosh and I could not contain our happiness. Her presence was indeed a blessing in the solitude of Elahiyeh. She asked us to go swimming in the pool on Amanieh Hill. Siranoush and I had our bathing trunks on.

Meanwhile, Turan took a rope to tie to our arms so she could lift us up in case we were drowning. Siranoush and Kourosh couldn't climb the steep slope of Amanieh Hill like I did, so we started from the low hills and slowly climbed up to reach the pool.

The Amanieh Hill pool was mostly used by foreigners, especially Americans. Tall white women with nice legs swam happily in the pool and then relaxed in Amanieh cafeteria, or sunbathed on beach chairs by the pool. Despite my young age, I watched them and admired their beauty. They were mostly accompanied by their boyfriend, husband or girlfriends.

The day we arrived at the pool, it was empty. We took off our clothes next to it. Turan tied the rope to Siranoush's arm. We entered the water at its lowest part. Since I did not know how to swim yet, I held the bar on the edge of the pool and constantly dipped my head in the water.

Turan stood by the pool and let us swim in the water and dip our heads in it. Then she put the little Kourosh into the water. He, too, started moving his arms and legs in the water with pleasure. Then she tied the rope to my arm, and I entered the pool area and started swimming in the water. Turan splashed water on me while Siranoush was holding fast to the bar of the edge of the pool and moved her legs in the water.

Meanwhile, I kept on swimming and dipping my head in the water and brought it up again to refresh my breath. At times, Turan pushed me into the water with her hand on my head and lifted it off to let me raise my head and breathe again. We all laughed and were happy. But once she put her hand on my head and did not lift. No matter how hard I tried to free my head to get to the top of the water, it was not possible.

I stopped breathing. I turned my head left and right, but no! Her hand was still there, preventing me from getting out of the water. Turan thought she was playing with us, but she seemed to have lost count and did not know that my tolerance underwater was limited. If she stopped me from getting my head out again, I would drown in the water.

I was holding my breath in my chest. Running out of tolerance, I was about to breathe in the water and my eyes were blurred. At the last moment, when I was feeling really bad, Turan removed her hand from my head. I quickly pulled my head out of the water and started coughing and breathing. I saw Turan, Siranush and Kourosh laughing. They still did not realise that if I did not get enough oxygen for a few moments, I would drown in the water.

After this incident, I came out of the water. I did not want to swim anymore. I coughed as if water had run down my nose and throat. Turan closed the swimming program, and we headed north to Amanieh Hill, which overlooked our house. Our house was right behind the hill.

There, they had placed a see-saw, swings and a carousel for kids and adults to play. Apart from the carousel, they charged each person 5–10 Tumans to play there for as long as he or she wished. Turan paid for us, and we entered the compound. We played there for an hour. Then we headed home sliding from behind the hill overlooking our garden house.

Visiting Dolatshahi Private Zoo

One Friday at sunset, my father drove the whole family in his army jeep from our garden to Dolatshahi Private Zoo, which was located on the left side of Pahlavi Street further up Vanak Sq., where they later built the Shahanshahi Park (now Mellat Park) on its opposite side. My father told us that the zoo was recently opened (in 1958) by a man named Mohammad Hossein Dolatshahi. Until then, I knew the animals from the Russian circuses that were often performed in Tehran. Its entrance was decorated with two golden lions. We went for a walk through the garden.

There were gardens full of colourful rose bushes, boxwoods and fruit trees on both sides of us. Everything was clean, new and tastefully decorated. Along the two sides of the sidewalk, lamps of different colours were installed in a row, the light of which later added to the splendour of the garden and illuminated it like the sun. The garden was irrigated and looked like a forest full of plants, and the scent of flowers and seedlings caressed the nose.

Inside the gardens, there were cages of various birds such as peacocks, colourful parrots, lovebirds, crowned cranes, various nightingales, pelicans, pheasants, eagles, vultures and hawks. It was there that I first met the hawk for the first time.

They attacked our pigeons at the railway house and injured and even ate them.

We walked along the sidewalk that led to the cage of a thick-necked snake. There was a junction there. One way went to the right and the other to the left. On both sides, there were cages of lions, tigers, leopards, bears, foxes, wolves, monkeys, deer, rams, giraffes, elks, ostriches, turtles and other animals. Signs urged visitors not to feed birds or animals at all. I understood the meaning of this request later because some visitors put a glass or needle or something dangerous in the food and endangered the animal's health.

We ended our tour by standing in front of each cage and watching the bird or animal with great pleasure. Returning from the front of the snake cage, we encountered a painful scene. The animal feeder had thrown a live white rabbit into a snake cage. The snake was slowly swallowing the poor rabbit from its head in front of us children. As a child, I was very upset by this zoo practice.

There was no reason to feed animals with living creatures in front of children and adults. It seems that later, the stench of animal faeces, abnormal noises and the escape of some predators, and even the high traffic of visitors caused the neighbours of the zoo to complain, which resulted in moving it to another place on Karaj Road.

The Master Thieves of Elahiyeh

Our place in Elahiyeh was the dream of professional thieves, where most affluent and wealthy families lived. Now our family was among them, even though my father wasn't very rich. To the south of the building, Mohammad had paved a terrace-like area with mosaics. During summers, we slept outside on the terrace in front of the building. Ashraf always spread our bedding there on the floor. It was late 1956 and there weren't many families living around us.

One night, I was sleeping as usual a little further away from the building close to the edge of the terrace. Ashraf was sleeping about 2 metres away from me near the building. Kourosh, Siranoush and Mohammad were sleeping next to her in a row. It was cloudy and windy. I'd covered my head with linen so it wouldn't get wet if it rained.

Suddenly, I heard a footstep by my side. It couldn't be anyone but a thief. Now I couldn't decide whether to pretend that I was sleeping until the thief left, or get up and start shouting. In the latter case, the thief might have beaten me, injured me, or strangled me. I wasn't close enough to my mother to get her up with the touch of my hand.

It seemed that the thief had entered our house from the opposite wall. Fear overcame me. I did not make a sound. I waited until Ashraf coughed and moved in the middle of her sleep, and then I ran to her. I told her that a thief had come.

Then I got inside the building. My mother, disturbed by my rapid movement, asked: 'What's happened? Where are you going?'

I said: 'The thief had come over my head.'

She woke Mohammad up immediately. They both looked in the dark inside the garden and in front of the building. They did not find anything. Mohammad said: 'We have two dogs. If someone comes, they'll wake us up.'

Of the two dogs, one was a small female dog named Bobby, who was especially mine, and the other was an old and disabled German shepherd whose horrible barking voice glorified him only. But Mohammad did not know that when we slept at night, they also slept, and when we got up, they also got up. Neither of them would be useful to us. They were just a hobby in our garden house.

After the thief incident, Mohammad hired Hossein Aqa as a gardener for our garden house. He was a tall and strong young man about 23 years old, from Kuhdasht, Lorestan. He had not served the army, because he was considered the breadwinner of his old father. He explained to me that every year he came to Tehran early in spring, worked and returned to Lorestan at the end of summer.

He only had his father. His mother had died many years ago. He jumped to and from in the garden like a wild and intoxicated horse with youthful energy. This time, he'd come to Tehran to work and save his money so he could return to his village to marry the village chief's daughter.

The girl's love had made Hossein happy and excited. His hair was dripping with sweat on his forehead, making him look even wilder. In the mornings he'd come out of his room on the west side of the hall to buy bread for us. Then he started watering the flowers and trees in the garden twice with a water can. In the evenings, after I'd finished my games and he'd watered the flowers and trees, we'd sit with him on the terrace of the building, and he'd tell me about his village in Lorestan.

The interesting thing for me was that he said: 'Most of the rural workers who work in Tehran go back to their villages on foot to save money. Some people really do not have the money to pay for their travel fare and have to choose the walking.' He continued: 'The road is more difficult on the way from Tehran to Qom and sometimes it continues to Isfahan.

'They keep walking for the love of their province day and night and move forward and do not think about rest and sleep. At night, on the way in the dark, they hear strange noises around them due to lack of sleep. Some people go crazy with fear. It seems to them that someone is talking to them in the dark.'

Hossein Aqa talked a lot about these dangers along the way. It usually took them 10–20 days depending on the distance to get home.

Meanwhile, Mohammad bought a jeep without having a driver's licence. We mostly drove to the city to Mahmoud's to see the family or go to the cinema or theatre. One night, when we returned home, Hossein Aqa started shouting and complaining, with a trembling voice, about why we had come home late and that we had left him alone in that remote and isolated place, at that time of night. Mohammad asked him the story.

With a confused and nervous face, he said: 'It was close to sunset. I had finished watering the garden and was sitting on the terrace, drinking tea. Suddenly, I looked down at the garden. I saw a few heads looking down at the garden from the wall and moving towards the north. It was as if they wanted to come to the building from the stairs on the north side of the garden. I got up and went to them and shouted: Who are you? What are you doing there?'

They answered: 'Don't make a noise, or we'll kill you.'

At that time, Hossein Aqa shouted because he was very scared and said: 'Now I'll show you all who wants to kill me.'

He ran to his shovel, picked it up and rushed to the thieves. The thieves, who were mostly short in stature and looked like chickens, fled from the shouts, shovel and the tall stature of Hossein Aqa, to the wall of the garden and threw themselves to the other side which was a vast plain.

Mohammad comforted him and promised not to be late for home anymore. My father was upset by what had happened. He turned to us and said: 'These useless dogs did not even make a fuss to make us happy. Wow, look what creatures we keep here!'

The next day he took the German shepherd with him and gave it to a friend as a gift. He told me: 'Now we have to choose another dog that can scare the thieves and make at least a noise with its barking at night.'

I was coming home from school one day. On the hills below Amanieh, I saw a large, pale yellow dog with severed ears that had apparently been cut. It was a smart and clever dog and ran back and forth like sheepdogs. I gave it a little of the bread I had taken to school with me, in my bag, to eat. He made friends with me at once and accompanied me home.

The next day, I saw him again in the hills. Seeing me, he came to me. Apparently, he was a stray dog that liked to walk with me. I brought him home and gave him some bread and water. He also became friends with my white Bobby dog, and they spent all the time together.

The next day, Mohammad examined him before going to his office. He said: 'It is a good dog. We'll keep it.' Now, after school and having dinner, I'd go for a walk with him. His figure and barking were interesting and misleading.

One day our neighbour's gardener asked me: 'Where is your wolf dog, now?'

I replied: 'He did not have the courage, so we sent him away.'

'So you think your new dog is brave?' he said sarcastically.

I answered: 'Our dogs are now in charge of guarding our home. In the middle of the night, if the sound of thieves approaching us is heard, Bobby starts barking with another dog.'

At the end of the summer of 1956, Hossein Aqa settled his account with Mohammad and was paid. Mohammad also paid him a large amount as a reward, and Hossein Aqa left for Kuhdasht in his province. Mohammad wouldn't usually do such things, but because he knew that Hossein Aqa needed money for his wedding, he helped him. Before he left, I asked whether he'd go on foot or by bus. He said that he'd go by bus because his fiancée was waiting for him to arrive soon for their wedding.

After Hossein Aqa left us, Mohammad hired another gardener named Haidar, who was from "Nain" and was about 26 years old. The new gardener lacked the strength and stamina of Hossein Aqa and needed us to tell him about his duties. He stayed with us for three weeks and then he left for his province because of his mother's illness.

He went to Mohammad's office near sunset to be paid for his work and came back to us to collect his belongings. Ashraf asked him to stay for the night, but he thanked her and said that he was going to visit his friends and stay with them. Then he left.

Meanwhile, Ashraf Khanum, the wife of my mother's cousin, had come to stay with us for a few days, on the weekend. My mother received her with pleasure, and they spent a happy time talking and laughing with each other and enjoyed being together. They kept talking until late at night, and when Mohammad returned home from work, he also joined in their conversation. He'd get a half-finished bottle of liquor at home to drink with Ashraf Khanum and insisted to fill up her glass, but she'd refuse because she wasn't used to it and didn't like it much. However, he poured some into her glass which she mixed with coca cola before drinking.

Then they'd start laughing loud together and the sound of their laughter filled our house with a pleasant and happy mood. Ashraf Khanum slept on the east side of the hall in our room with Siranoush, I and Nanneh Jan, while Kourosh, Ashraf and Mohammad slept in the other room on the southeast of the hall.

That day, after Haidar left, at the end of the night, everyone finally went to bed and slept. In the middle of the night, we woke up to a terrible sound coming from the kitchen. Ashraf Khanum went to my mother's room and asked her about the sound. My mother did not know what had happened.

Then they both turned on the oil lamps, and together, they went to the kitchen to find the cause of the sound. It took a while, but they didn't come. Curiosity caused me to follow them. I saw them both coming out of the kitchen. They had not found anything suspicious there.

Everything looked safe and sound, but they still had not found the answer to the question of what caused the horrible noise. Finally, my mother said, 'A cat may have entered the kitchen through the small window or a pan may have fallen to the ground.'

In that sleepy state, no one followed the cause of the sound. We all went back to bed and slept.

The next morning, Nanneh Jan (my mother's grandmother) went to the kitchen to make tea and prepare breakfast for us. She saw that the window glass had been smashed, and the fragments were scattered on the floor, and the samovar, all the pans and cooking utensils and the dishes were taken away. The kitchen was literally stripped bare. She immediately woke my mother up and told her the story. We all just realised that the terrible sound that night was due to a broken window hit with a stone.

In that dim light, Ashraf and Ashraf Khanum did not notice the broken window and the pieces of glass on the floor. Apparently, the thieves outside waited for us to sleep again to start their theft. Fortunately, our primus stove was still in place. Thieves might have forgotten to take it, too. My mother boiled some water in a bowl and gave me and Siranush bread, cheese and tea before going to school. After we left, Ashraf borrowed two small and large pans from Mehri Khanum, the maid of that English family, to cook lunch for us.

Mohammad was very upset about this event. Mehri Khanum called the police station at my mother's request. Immediately, several trained and specialised theft agents came. Our area was the residence of the nobles and aristocrats of Tehran, especially since the house of Mrs Fakhr al-Dowleh was close to ours, the local police station was very much on the alert and watchful.

The police inspected the kitchen and the garden. Mohammad had made a small garden that started from the big door and ended at the end of the building, on the right side of the gate, in which he'd just sowed some flower seeds which hadn't yet germinated. He used to water it regularly. The officers recognised the footprint of "Giveh" (a kind of handmade shoes worn by peasants in Iran) in this garden, which belonged to the thief.

Mohammad informed them that Haidar was paid for his job and left the day before. Officers became suspicious. They got the address of his friend from Mohammad and found Haidar in a very short time. They brought him to our house and compared the footprints in the garden with his Giveh. Unfortunately, they matched.

Haidar swore that he was not a thief and that the footprints did not belong to him. Officers pushed him forward and told Mohammad that he would be taken to the police station to confess. Haidar cried as he left the big door and asked Mohammad for help. Mohammad thought that his kitchen utensils were not worth imprisoning his gardener for them. Particularly, Haidar was supposed to go to his village to his mother that day. So Mohammad told the officers to release him.

When I came home from school that day, I saw that the window glass was fixed and that they had bought new kitchen utensils. The smell of a delicious "Qormeh Sabzi" (an Iranian dish), which was also cooking on the oil stove, filled the air. Mohammad was busy talking with the police all morning, and he went in his jeep to buy kitchen utensils together with Ashraf and Ashraf Khanum.

My mother returned the pans to Martin's family with a box of sweets and a big thank you. Mohammad kept complaining that he was out of work and life that day, but there was no way out. In that remote area, without a shop or a bazaar nearby, Mohammad could only buy everything in Tajrish as soon as possible.

Mehri Khanum, the maid of the English family, was very kind to us who used their phone regularly. Mohammad asked Ashraf to ask Mehri Khanum to call his office and tell his secretary that he would go there in the afternoon. Maybe by the order of Martin's wife, Linda, Mehri Khanum picked up a few cans of pineapples and mandarins from the English family's cabinet and brought them to us. Siranush, Kourosh and I ate it with pleasure.

Photo No. 25: Linda (the English neighbour of the author in Elahiyeh) with her daughter and son (1957).

After Haidar left, this time my mother Ashraf tried to bring a new servant to buy at least our bread and grocery from Arbab Jamshid's shop for her, on Fereshteh Street.

Finally, a 17-year-old boy was found in the vicinity of Amanieh Hill. He was a well-spoken chap from Ardabil, about 165 cm tall, and his name was Rasoul. He knew how to please people. It was as if he was looking for a job since he went from house to house asking if they wanted a worker or a servant.

When he knocked on our door and asked Ashraf about it, she happily said: 'Yes, we need a servant. Come here tonight and talk with my husband.'

He came that night and talked with Mohammad who also liked him a lot. The following day, he started working at our house. After coming home from school, I'd sit with him on the terrace, and he talked to me about himself and his life.

Ashraf gave him some money every morning to buy bread, cheese, butter, eggs and other items from the grocery store on the street. Aqa Reza also brought us milk on his cart in the evenings. My mother boiled it on the lamp stove and let it cool down for the next morning.

Rasoul was working at our house for the fourth day. Early in the morning, Ashraf gave him a 20 Tuman banknote to go shopping for us. He went when I was at school. Ashraf explained to me that Rasoul returned empty-handed a few hours later and said, in a disturbed state, that he had lost his money along the way. Ashraf was very upset. She told him: 'What should I do now? How can I cook for the children?'

Twenty Tumans was worth a lot of money at that time and could not be easily ignored.

Ashraf went to Mehri Khanum to give a call there to Mohammad. Mohammad immediately got in his jeep and came home. He slapped Rasoul angrily and took him by the hand and dragged him along to the police station on Amanieh Street, which was in front of Amanieh Hill. There he said: 'This rogue boy has stolen our 20 Tumans.'

Rasoul was also beaten at the police station, and they tried to get him to confess what he had done with that 20 Tumans. The officer then asked Mohammad to consent to the boy's release. He said that in case he didn't, the boy would be sent to the court the next day, and they'd send him to the youth detention centre where he'd be even better trained as a thief, and his future would be ruined as a result. He further continued: 'Now he may have become a little bit human with the beatings he has received in the meantime, but no one will be his opponent after his term of imprisonment.'

Mohammad agreed. The police officer released Rasoul. A few weeks later, Ashraf heard from women in the neighbourhood that a young man had worked for them for a few days as a servant and a gardener, and then their gold, jewellery and cash were all lost at once. The character she talked about was similar to Rasoul's. Ashraf was happy that she'd just lost 20 Tumans.

One day in summer, my aunt Tahereh, who was now called Iran, came to see us. This was her first visit to our garden house. Ashraf spread her bedding next to the window of our living room and Siranush slept next to her. Nanneh Jan and I slept on the other side of the room. To keep the night from getting too dark in the room, they just lowered the wick of the kerosene lamp to give the room some light.

It was almost half an hour after sleeping when one of the thieves came in from the window, put one foot in the middle of Iran's bed, bent down and turned off the light so that he would not be recognised stealing in the dark. Iran and Siranush saw the thief move, but they were so afraid of his action that they did not dare to shout. Half an hour after the thief left, Iran ran to the room of my parents who were sleeping. She shouted: 'A thief has come! A thief has come!'

We all got up and ran out of the rooms, but there was no news of the thief. We went back to sleep. Unfortunately, on the first day of her visit, a thief came to our house.

Fortunately, the thief did not seem to find anything useful with us and went about his business empty-handed. My father checked with the neighbours and the local police station and concluded that most of the thieves were the same workers who worked around our house.

One day Ashraf, Mohammad and I went to the city. Nanneh Jan, Siranush and little Kourosh stayed at home. When we came back, Nanneh Jan was very upset. She said: 'From seven o'clock at night, the thieves were hiding in the dark on the tall trees behind our house (their branches had also grown to our garden) and whistled at each other.'

Siranush said: 'Nanneh Jan herself took a cane in her hand and went out with a lamp.'

She continued that Nanneh Jan shouted in front of the building: 'Hossein, Hassan, Akbar. Come! Thieves are entering the garden and the building from the trees. Be quick!' Then she said that the whistling sound stopped, and they heard the thieves coming down from the trees, jumping down and running away.

Photo No. 26: Nanneh Jan, the grandmother of the author's mother in her sixties.

Turan (my other aunt) married Fereydoun Nasehi in the fall of 1955, at the house of my uncle Mahmoud. Fereydoun Khan took his wife to his parents after their wedding. They lived on Heshmat al-Dowleh Street. We hadn't visited them since their wedding ceremony. Mohammad made an excuse that he didn't have enough money to buy them a present and that we could not go to them empty-handed. It took him a year to finally decide to take us to them.

Meanwhile, Turan gave birth to his son, Farhad, in September 1956. Now Mohammad had a good reason to buy a baby carriage for their son. He bought it together with Ashraf from the Pirayesh shop in Lalehzar, and we all went to the house of Turan and Fereydoun Khan with a box of sweets. Only Nanneh Jan was left alone at home.

Turan was very happy to see us. They treated us very well to a great dinner. Turan made a kind of Baadkubeh dish for us that she had learnt from her mother-in-law. Mohammad liked it very much and always talked about it. There, I got to meet Fereydoun Khan's young son from his first wife.

He had long and wide ears like his grandfather's. Mohammad believed that he'd become somebody important in future because of his God-given talent. That's because Mohammad claimed to know people's character from their appearance. We later saw that this boy became one of the most stupid sons of Fereydoun Khan.

At 10:30 at night, we finally left Turan's house. We were all fine and happy. I, in particular, was feeling very good due to this meeting. We drove up the steep Pahlavi Street in Mohammad's jeep, pressing the accelerator and changing gears a lot. We entered the house tired and exhausted, at last.

Immediately, we took out our clothes and put them on chairs in the hall and went to sleep in our beddings which Nanneh Jan had spread for us on the terrace in front of the building. In the early hours of the morning, we woke up to the shouts of Nanneh Jan saying: 'O God! Oh, five Holy Saints! Oh, Mohammad!'

She was holding a kerosene lamp in her hand. Ashraf ran to her and asked what the matter was. Nanneh Jan said: 'Thieves have taken everything with them. I heard their voice coming from the rooftop, but when I reached there, they'd gone.'

Immediately, I went to the rooftop with my mother and father. The door was open. There was a brick wall going down parallel to the right-hand side of Fereshteh Street that led to our wall. Behind that wall, before our rooftop, there was a bare land where we played, which was not planted yet. Right where the two walls met, there stood a crowbar (used for moving heavy objects).

Mohammad examined it closely. I wanted to take it, but he stopped me saying: 'Don't touch it. You might remove the fingerprints of thieves on it.'

It was still dawn and the sun rays had just started to shine. Ashraf ran to the house of the English family at once and called Mehri, who was living in her small room, from outside. The poor girl got up and heard the story. She called the police.

Meanwhile, Linda got up, too, because of the talking noise between Mehri and Ashraf. She asked Mehri what the matter was. We were all upset. In 10 minutes, a police jeep with three officers arrived. Before their arrival, Ashraf and Mohammad summed up what the thieves had taken.

All the carpets in the hall and the carpet in Mohammad and Ashraf's room, as well as all the clothes they'd put on the chairs in the hall at night and even the wardrobe clothes in their room. They were all looted. Ashraf lamented because, in addition to her clothes, the thieves had taken with them the jewels she had worn and placed on the table in the hall, before sleeping. In short, they had stripped us naked.

Seeing this situation, Ashraf shouted at Mohammad: 'Oh man, look where you've brought us to! We are robbed all the time.'

On the other hand, Nanneh Jan's voice suddenly rose. She shouted: 'The thieves have stolen my shroud. It was in my bag, and they took it away. What should I do now without a shroud?'

Nanneh Jan shouted and grumbled so much that Mohammad got angry. He said: 'I do not say anything about all these expensive carpets and jewellery that were stolen from us. Now you are making so much noise for a few metres of your shroud! Do not be sad! Do not grieve. I will buy you a new shroud.'

The thieves were apparently looking for a tablecloth or cloth to put small items in to take away. The shroud was several metres long and was useful for this purpose.

The officers came. They started their investigation from the rooftop. They took away the crowbar. One of them said that this was the work of professional thieves. The officer did not waste any more time and hurried to the hills south of our building to look for the thieves.

I was so shocked and anxious that I forgot to go with him and show him the way, particularly the cave I'd found a few days ago in the hills that could help them find the thieves. I had walked south through the hills and knew them well. I even walked around that place every few days. I was sure that the thieves had hidden the heavy carpets in that cave and had escaped themselves so that they could move them later. The officer went and disappeared behind the hill in our view.

Now we only hoped that he would find the thieves and take our property back from them. But after 30 minutes, tired and exhausted, he returned empty-handed. His search did not yield any results, although it had taken a long time.

I might have been neglectful to chase the thieves. Seeing that crowbar and hearing the words of Nanneh Jan saying the thieves had just jumped out of the wall and started running with the stolen property when she came to the rooftop, made me think of running after them at that moment. Those thieves wanted to either hide the stolen property in that cave or take themselves to that main street (Old Shemiran Road). That street was far from our area. Thieves could not easily escape with the heavy carpets and other property.

Fear, however, overcame me, because it was very dangerous to pursue them alone and stand against those professional thieves who must have been stronger than me and probably carried cold weapons with them, too. The next few days, as I walked that path, I wondered how the thieves were able to lift all that load up and down the hills by hand. The distance was very long, even to that cave.

The officers recorded all the details of the theft and estimated that the number of thieves with the amount of property they'd stolen should have been four to five. Ashraf wondered about how the thieves pulled the carpets out from under the table and chairs in the hall and from under the wardrobe of Ashraf and Mohammad's room and took them away without making a noise. Nanneh Jan believed: 'They must have sprayed something in the air to put us to sleep.'

The thieves had come to the building through the backyard, even though the door was closed from the inside. It was as if they had cunningly opened the back door from the outside and entered the building without making a noise. They knew exactly where we slept.

They did not come to Nanneh Jan's room or to the terrace of the building where we slept. It was obvious that they had been watching us for some time. Police officers left our home with regret after they investigated into the theft and wrote their report. Nanneh Jan made us breakfast.

Now Ashraf and Mohammad were faced with a new dilemma. Thieves had taken all their clothes. Mohammad, particularly, did not have anything to wear to go to his office. Ashraf again went to the kind, Assyrian Mehri Khanum and told her the story. Mehri also told the problem to the English woman, Linda.

A few minutes later, we saw that Mehri brought some of Martin's clothes and some women's shirts for Ashraf. She told Ashraf: 'The English couple are very upset and sympathise with you for what's happened to you. They've given you these clothes so you can at least wear them today before buying new ones.'

Mohammad looked very funny in Martin's suit with baggy legs because Martin was a tall and wide man. Linda's clothes, however, fitted Ashraf's height and size exactly.

From then on, a friendship started between Linda and Ashraf, even though my mother did not speak English. When Linda and her husband and children were out of their house, Siranush and I and sometimes Ashraf went to see Mehri at the English family home. Martin worked for an oil company. He had a family black Console Ford with the word "service" written on the back plate. There was nothing special in their house.

The only thing that caught my eye was their toilet, which was between the living room and the bedroom. It was a foreign-style toilet with a small bookshelf placed in front of it. Most of the books there were novels. I'd just started learning English in the seventh grade with Mohammad Sadeq Iraji. So I looked at the English books with a strange interest. Visiting the English family toilet that day was a lesson for me because it was there that I realised that one can also use one's time to read books and learn more, even in the restroom.

One day Mehri came to us. 'Last night, Martin and Linda talked about Iran,' she said.

'Then Martin told me that the Iranians are warm and hardworking people, but he would not understand why this land does not develop with this good and persistent nation." Ashraf told to Mohammad at night.

He listened to it all. Then he said: 'Tell this English man to shut up! This is none of his business!'

But, after he calmed down, he said: 'It seems like our English neighbour is only doing his own business and doesn't know much about other things. Tell him to read a little about the history of Britain's relations with Iran. There he finds his answer!'

But this answer was expressed at a party by an American expert of the Office of Principle Four, after completing his service in Iran, before leaving the country. He said: 'All during my service in your country, I faced a puzzle which I'm not sure if I can ever solve, and perhaps the Iranians themselves will not be able to understand the root cause of this great defect. Iranians are very precise and intelligent. They think well; they plan well; and they carefully distinguish between the good and the bad, but they do not carry out these effective plans and schemes. It is like I see my wallet falling from my pocket on the street but don't take a step to pick it up!

'The government, for instance, is sure that if it is careful in collecting taxes and real taxes from the rich, a budget deficit will be (overcome or eliminated) provided, but it does not do so. The municipality knows well that if it does not cause unnecessary problems for the people and leaves them free, they will keep their streets and neighbourhoods cleaner than the municipality workers, but it causes problems for the people on all sides and even refuses their free help. The Ministry of Finance is sure that if it assigns embezzlers to carry out important transactions such as buying grain, etc., they will abuse their position, but it will still commission them.

'In Iran, mining engineers are appointed by the accounting department and accountants are appointed to be in charge of weather and meteorological conditions, or are responsible for irrigation! In an office that only needs seven or eight people to do the job, 80 people are employed for no reason, and conversely, for an office that needs more members, a small number is considered.'

The American expert said, 'I do not know the reason for these inverted actions and why you do not walk in the right and rational way?'

He continued: 'A few months ago, one of my colleagues was commissioned to establish a classification organisation with the help of knowledgeable and insightful members of the Iranian government. The purpose of establishing this organisation was to give each employee a job that he could do. A member who specialises in recruitment will take on the same duties, and someone who knows forestry should be employed for that job. Although there is still a small organisation called Job Classification, it will certainly remain useless like other useful programs because such an action has a tremendous effect on improving the situation of offices and is a kind of profound administrative transformation.

'For this reason, no step will ever be taken to put this useful plan into action. If a group of businessmen gather together and want to start a factory that meets the needs of the people in terms of essential household items like plates, bowls and the like, the more they hesitate to issue a permit, the more problems are created for this group and they finally give up. Considering this all, give me the right to say that I do not know why useful work should not be done in your country, and without exception, public benefit projects remain stagnant and will be archived. But if there is a suggestion that 300 electric fans are needed for such and such office, that is, three or four fans for each room, this will be implemented step by step, and they will immediately buy the fans that are not really needed as many, at that high price.

'No civilised or backward country is as generous as Iranians in terms of extravagance and wages. This is an unsolved mystery that no one can solve, and I do not know why you are working so diligently on something that does not benefit you.' Taken from Ettela'at newspaper "Talks of an American" Tuesday, 20 February 1954, page five.

The American officer working for Principle Four, himself, may not have known at all that the confusion and incompetence in the Iranian administration was a direct result of long-term foreign policy and US intervention in all of Iran's affairs to control it without the need for recruiting troops and engaging in hostilities.

For example, at least 80% of the officers who came to Iran to take care of the country's health were retired personnel. It was later known that the American advisers themselves serving in Iran were mostly sergeants who had fought in Korea or Vietnam, were disabled or retired from the regiment and were assigned to non-specialist disciplines. If anything of importance was done in Iran, it was more due to the Budget and Planning Organisation, not to the Truman Four principle. American sergeants and advisers in Iran were unorganised and lacked experience and followed the same method of confusion. Quote from Biglarbeigi:

> In our Department of Agriculture, there was a sergeant who was constantly drunk and did not know anything. They had set a budget for him and he got a good salary. In addition he received a "right to savagery" because they believed that he worked in a wild country. The judge who had a bachelor's degree in law and justice was assigned as the head of the warehouse of the agricultural industry.

A week had passed since our house was robbed. Mohammad bought new clothes for himself and my mother. He sent Martin's clothes to the laundry and then returned them through Mehri to the English family in a beautiful package, together with a large box of premium pistachios to express his gratitude. Mohammad did not know English, but he told Mehri to thank Martin on his behalf. Ashraf, however, kept Linda's clothes.

The question for me was why the thieves did not ambush the English house. Mehri told me that Martin has a pistol at home to defend himself and his family and that where it was kept was known to everyone to use it in an emergency.

Perhaps the thieves knew about the existence of guns in the foreigners' homes and that's why they left them unharmed.

Two weeks later, I was leaving home one morning for Pahlavi Street. I suddenly saw Mr Bina, the northern neighbour of our house, holding the hand of a young and sleepy man, and while whistling the guard's whistle, he moved down Fereshteh Street towards Pol-e Rumi. Constables usually used that whistle to inform each other and get in touch. Mr Bina had recently moved to the new house he'd built for his family on the corner of Fereshteh and Fakhr al-Dowleh streets. The young man showed no resistance. I asked Mr Bina about the story.

He said that the young man was a thief. Then continued: 'He robbed our house last night with his friends who have taken away our property. However, as he was tired, he wanted to take a rest behind our wall and there he fell asleep.'

The young man insisted that he was a worker and not a thief and that he was just sleeping behind the wall. I went on with my way. I don't know how the incident ended, but deep down inside, I laughed at Mr Bina who was playing like artists at that time of the day, looking for a constable. I'd never seen a constable guarding our area up until then.

Mohammad's Effective Solution to Get Rid of Elahiyeh Thieves

The robbery had upset Mohammad. He was constantly thinking about it. From his angry look, one could guess that he was determined to find a way to get the thieves out of our house for good. He himself was also in danger. My mother once said that even my father had noticed several thieves at his head while sleeping on the terrace at night, but he did not move because he was afraid that the thieves would harm him and all of us for some trivial furniture.

One day Mohammad complained angrily: 'Why are we not living in peace here? Why don't these thieves leave us alone? We are all in trouble, all in harassment and all in financial loss! There is also no help from the local police to clear the thieves from our neighbourhood.'

Then he continued: 'Wow, what antic dogs we have that do not even make a noise when the thieves come, to at least make us happy.'

It really was like that. The dogs were used to our way of living. They put their head between their legs and slept when we went to bed and got up with us the next morning. They weren't bothered by the talk of the thieves among themselves. They slept carefree, regardless of where the thieves came from, which was the rooftop this time. Mohammad was so angry with them that he kicked Bobby and that useless yellow dog, with its impressive figure, out of the house at once.

The yellow dog immediately disappeared. He must have tied himself to another family, but Bobby stayed behind. He was wagging his tail as we opened and closed the entrance door. It was until one day when I saw a man in a car who liked Bobby. Apparently, he was waiting to see someone coming out of our house.

The moment he saw me, he asked: 'Is this beautiful dog that's constantly moving behind the door of your house, yours?'

I said: 'It was, but not anymore. My father no longer wants him. He prefers to have a German shepherd.'

He then asked: 'Could I have it then?'

I answered: 'Yes! By all means.'

He got out of his car, looked carefully at Bobby a bit and then opened the back door of his car, picked Bobby up and put him in the car. Bobby showed no resistance when he took him away. In this way, we got rid of two lazy and good-for-nothing dogs. I noticed that Mohammad himself was then trying to find a dog to handle all the thieves.

**Photo No. 27: Mohammad (Author's father)
at the age of 42 (1958).**

"Ziba" Our Antic Dog

A few days passed. Mohammad arrived in a taxi at lunch. He pulled out a skinny, yellow dog from the back of the taxi. It had vomited there. The driver was shouting in anger, but Mohammad paid his fare with an extra for washing his car and calmed him down.

Ashraf took a look at the dog and said: 'Was there a dog shortage there? Couldn't you find anything better? What do we want a sick dog for?'

Mohammad told her that the dog's father was a wolf and his mother a dog. He also added that he had a lot of trouble finding it and had paid a lot to buy him.

Mohammad then took the dog to the lower garden and tied it with a rope to a tree, on the east side of the garden, under the branches of the walnut trees that had overgrown above our garden and cast a shadow.

As Mohammad was telling me about the dog seller, it suddenly threw up in its sickness and made both of us upset. Mohammad himself did not like the situation. He might have concluded that the seller had actually deceived him and given him a dying sick dog. All at once, I brought the dog a bowl of water and put it in front of him. Mohammad said: 'We shouldn't give him anything now, because he has diarrhoea.'

I, however, brought him some alfalfa from the neighbour's field and placed it next to him to eat if he wanted and cleanse his stomach.

After we had lunch, Mohammad said: 'How do you like this dog to be called Ziba?'

I said it was alright. The same night, Mohammad brought a collar for Ziba so it wouldn't be hurt by the rope. Ziba only drank during the daytime, and Mohammad gave him a few spleens at night. He got them from a butcher on Shah Reza Street, near his office. Ziba loved to eat them.

As days passed by, Ziba gradually started to recover. His hair, which looked dull and lifeless, got smooth and shiny. I didn't much like to be with him. I was, in fact, afraid of him. Any time I got close to him, he snorted like a wolf, showing its teeth by raising his snout ready to attack me, but then he'd calm down and wag his tail.

He didn't drink water like a real dog. Instead, he bit and swallowed it. He howled instead of barking. Workers, farmers and the thieves around were alarmed to see that a wolf was suddenly found in our area. Now everybody was really scared.

Mohammad sold his old jeep and looked for a new military one. For this reason, he'd take a bus from his office to the beginning of Fereshteh Street and then walk home from there. He would return home earlier for Ziba's sake. Long before he'd walked down Fereshteh Street, Ziba could sense him coming and start exciting sounds of howling and barking while jumping towards the door. He'd try to get himself rid of the clutches of the collar to welcome Mohammad.

Hearing his noise, we knew that Mohammad was approaching. Had he been driving his jeep home, Ziba would have sensed it from the roar of its engine. It had become a mystery to us how Ziba realised Mohammad's coming from that distance.

On the one hand, he was more than happy to get his daily ration of spleens in a few more minutes from Mohammad and on the other, seeing Mohammad, whom he loved, excited and pleased him. Mohammad played with him after having his meal. Then he walked with him around the garden and held his head between his palms and caressed it.

After Ziba's recovery, Mohammad moved him from the lower garden to the upper one and tied his collar chain to a long nail pounded into the ground, a couple of metres away from the entrance of the building. He wanted Ziba to be close to us. It was cool there in the mornings and evenings, but at noon, the sizzling sun badly scorched Ziba there, without a sunshade or canopy to protect him. Trying to free himself from the sun, he'd keep throwing himself at us such that the chain of the collar would be torn or the nail loosened. It was fixed again by Mohammad every night.

At times, when he managed to free himself, he would run around the building with boundless energy stored in him, or jump up the wall and get out of the building. We all ran away from him and were trapped inside the building at that time because none of us dared to leave the building and face him outside except my father. Almost once every two days, Mohammad came home with a new and stronger collar and confidently said: 'Ziba can no longer tear this one.'

But the next night when he came home, he was again faced with a torn collar.

At last, Mohammad ordered a strong collar for Ziba. They made it with several layers and put pieces of iron inside its fabric. It seemed that this collar worked for a while because

Ziba could not tear it easily anymore. He loved us so ardently that he jumped up on our arms and body and licked our faces with his tongue. At times, his leaps knocked us down to the ground. He was more accustomed to little Kourosh.

When seeing him, he ran around him and jumped on him such that Kourosh often fell to the ground. Screaming, Ashraf saved him from Ziba's hands. I had never seen a dog so hot and energetic until then.

In the meantime. Fereydoun Haqshenas, Ashraf's half-brother and my uncle, came to visit us from Rasht and stayed with us for a week. He made friends with Ziba from the very beginning of his arrival. Apparently, animals sense who to make friends with and quickly get along with. In the evenings, Fereydoun took the chain of Ziba's collar in his hand and the two of us went for walking with the dog.

Outside the house, whenever Ziba saw somebody, he wanted to rush to him and bite him, but Fereydoun held the chain firmly in his hand and stopped him. We walked on Fereshteh Street towards Pol-e Rumi with Ziba. Then we turned a complete semi-circle in the hills and plains around and walked to the back of Amanieh Hill. Fereydoun had become Ziba's coach, and Ziba really enjoyed the week that Fereydoun spent with him. Ziba's aggression was somehow relieved because of these daily walks around our garden house.

Now, looking at Ziba's fit and agile figure, we could see how fast he had grown up during that time. Apparently, he was just a puppy when he arrived at our house. Mohammad untied his collar chain during nights before going to bed, so he could go after the thieves. As he was tied all day long in one place, he was very happy when unleashed and ran like a released prisoner, out of joy, everywhere all through the night.

The arrival of Ziba solved the thieves' problem. Nobody dared to get close to our house and ambush it anymore. In addition, Ziba sometimes jumped off the wall and attacked everyone that he saw outside. Workers and farmers went home at most at eight o'clock after their daily work. So anybody outside in the middle of the night in that wasteland could be a thief.

Ziba's presence also caused us another problem. He'd learnt to jump off the wall to the other side. He'd occasionally tear off his strong collar, despite its tightness, during the day and leave the house. If he saw anyone on the street or on the hills, he would attack him and bite his arms and legs. No one knew that this wolf-like dog belonged to us, in the beginning. They all thought that a wolf had been found in our area.

One evening after watering the flowers, I was so exhausted and was drinking tea. I suddenly saw from the widow that Ziba was standing on the terrace to the east of the building, shaking his head. It seemed like he had torn his collar again which hurt his neck. He walked around the house a little and jumped off from the south wall to the other side of the building. I told Ashraf about it immediately.

She went to Mehri Khanum's door at once to call my father. Mohammad told Ashraf over the phone: 'Ziba does not hurt us. He just attacks the others. I'm busy right now. I'll buy a new collar at night and come home early.'

Ashraf returned home trembling with fear. Ziba was nowhere to be seen. An hour later, two workers knocked on our door. When I opened the door, I noticed that one of them had blood on his hands and arms, and his face looked pale with fear. Another worker was holding a spade in his hand. He said: 'I've come here to talk about your dog.'

I called my mother.

'Our master is not at home, right now,' she told the workers. 'There is nothing we can do about it. You can come at night and talk to him.'

They nagged and left unhappy. The moment my father arrived, Ziba also showed up. It was because Mohammad always brought his food with him. That night, Mohammad tied him with a new collar.

However, in an hour or two, he untied Ziba again to let him take care of the house. In the morning, before he went to his office, he tied the dog again. Again in the evening, Ziba freed himself and ignoring my whistles, he jumped over the wall and disappeared.

Two hours later, about seven or eight workers came to our door with spades and pickaxes. Again, Ziba had made some trouble chasing a frightened worker, who was running away from him. He'd reached out to him and bit his buttock with his sharp teeth. There was a riot in front of our house. Everyone was shouting.

They were moving their spades and pickaxes in the air. They wanted to kill Ziba. Ashraf tried to calm that angry crowd. She told them: 'We ourselves are tired of this dog. Come in two hours and talk to our master. He is not home yet.'

One of them said, 'Ma'am, what are you talking about? Your dog bites people and you do nothing about it. What does this mean?'

Workers were gathering all around the house for half an hour before they finally left. They did not return that night after Mohammad came home. I do not know what happened to that injured poor worker. Mohammad was so upset and angry with the thieves that he thought every worker and farmer was one of them and felt no sympathy for them when Ziba bit them. He said: 'Ziba is doing his job well.'

We got rid of the master thieves of Elahiyeh forever thanks to Ziba, our strong and brave dog. Maybe our neighbours, near and far, also benefitted from Ziba's presence, because we no longer heard of theft anywhere around us. However, we ourselves were not safe from Ziba's aggressive behaviour.

Sheep Breeding Experiment in Our Garden House and Ziba's Nuisance

It was a public holiday, one Thursday. With a previous agreement with a client, my father drove us to Ab-e Yek, in Qazvin, in his jeep to show him a property. Ab-e Yek was the place where my father worked as a district governor, when he was young. The property he wanted to sell to the customer was very large.

The owner had a large herd of goats and sheep that moved to the sunny plain from the green plain, accompanied by a few stubborn sheepdogs and returned noisily after a few hours before sunset. Mohammad and his client were so pleased to see all those fat and healthy goats and sheep and hear their noise which disturbed the peace and quiet of the place.

In the meantime, several people from Qazvin came in a van and bought 10 sheep and left. Mohammad immediately calculated if raising sheep in our house garden, on that 1,000 square metre land, would be profitable. We had alfalfa growing abundantly in the fields of Fakhr al-Dowleh, as well as the grass that grew around our house garden. One could use this for future milk, meat and skin and also sell the lambs.

Seeing that van's purchase, Mohammad got encouraged and dared to buy two male and female sheep to start with.

We put them behind the driver's seat. I sat next to them and brought the sheep home. My father tied them to the wall in the lower garden under the trees with a rope so that they would not damage our summer crops, flowers and trees during the day. He was sure that Ziba would not harm the two sheep. In fact, dogs support sheep instead of harassing them.

However, only a week later, Mohammad just realised that keeping sheep was not his kind of business. He could make more money selling property than raising sheep, of which he had no experience. It seemed like he mostly wanted to have fun than make money out of them. One afternoon, Ziba untied his collar and jumped off the wall and left. He came back after a while, and the first thing he did was attack the sheep.

With the screams and shouts of Ashraf and Nanneh Jan, Ziba left them alone and jumped out of the wall again and left. After his return, Mohammad tied Ziba with chains again. The next morning, he found out that Ziba had bitten one of the sheep's tail and slightly injured it. That morning he put one of the sheep in his jeep and took it away with him. At night, he told us that he'd sold it to a friend.

Mohammad handed the other sheep over to the butcher, who slaughtered it, and took its skin, intestines and abomasum with him for his payment. The next day, which was Friday, Mohammad had a big celebration by grilling mutton with family members in the backyard. Thus ended the breeding of sheep in our home garden.

Raising Chickens and Roosters Despite Ziba's Presence

It was the summer of 1957. I sometimes went to his office with Mohammad and stayed there all day and came home with him at night. One day he took me to the house of an army officer who had the rank of second lieutenant and was called "Zomorodian". He wanted to sell his house because he said it was too small for him, and now he was trying to find a house with a large yard on the way to Karaj. He had turned his current two-storey house into a chicken coop.

Everywhere I looked there were chickens moving around. He told Mohammad that he had been raising chickens for several years. He'd started with a chicken and a rooster, and now he owned about 1,500 chickens and roosters and wanted to leave the army and devote his entire time to his own chickens, which were also financially profitable. Mohammad was amazed at seeing all those chickens and roosters and hearing about the money being exchanged for their sale, especially their eggs. He promised Zomorodian to find him a small field on Karaj Road.

As we came out of his house, Mohammad told me: 'Dariush! Did you see how we've wasted our land? Our thousand-metre garden in Elahiyeh is just left useless, but smart people raise hens and roosters in their small house.'

The idea of raising chickens had previously occurred to Mohammad from his friend Jalal Farazi, who had started raising chickens in the basement of his house on Farvardin Street. However, Mohammad became so fascinated with poultry farming and chicken raising of the army officer, Zomorodian, that he immediately and eagerly made his final decision and acted swiftly. That night, he planned to build a large poultry house. The next day he went to Karaj, guided by his secretary, to buy the best chickens at that time which were known as "Kentucky". The hens were fat and pale red, and the roosters weighed several kilograms each. I had never seen roosters that big before.

The next morning, a carpenter came to us and built a few chicken coops with several nesting boxes, next to the west side wall of the lower garden. He made them so strong with high-quality wood that Ziba could not bother the hens and roosters. A truck came to our house after two days and delivered the chickens.

Soon after, Mohammad hired a man from Yazd, named "Khosrow Khan", to take care of the chickens and water the garden. Khosrow Khan started working, but he was very much afraid of Ziba from the first day. This made Ziba sensitive to him and rushed to him when he saw Khosrow Khan. Fortunately, Ziba was tied on a leash, and Khosrow Khan could easily do his job.

Mohammad was very happy and optimistic. He thought he could make a fortune with hens and roosters, but he had no experience raising chickens. He knew nothing about their diseases and how to cure them. He thought they'd graze in the garden and lay eggs effortlessly, and the eggs would hatch, so would the money. Less than two weeks after the arrival of the hens and roosters, I saw a few of them start to take a nap.

They closed their eyes and plunged their heads inside for a few minutes. During the day, they went up and down in the garden. Close to the sunset, Khosrow Khan would feed them with seeds and guide them to their coops.

Everything looked fine for the chickens. They had only one thing missing; we did not think about where the chickens should lay their eggs. They were miserable to find a place. They went everywhere to lay eggs. They came to the building to lay more eggs.

They laid eggs everywhere—even in the room to the right of the building we'd intended for the gardener. I followed them whenever I heard them cluck and picked the egg the moment they laid it. Every morning, we beat the egg yolk in a glass with sugar, mixed it with milk and at times cocoa and drank it with our breakfast.

One Thursday, I was reading the pamphlet "Attila" at home. The story was written by "Jalal Ne`matollahi" every week, and he added some other interesting topics to it as well, such that it became a book of almost 1,400 pages. Meanwhile, I suddenly noticed that Ziba had unleashed himself and was wandering angrily around the garden. He was in a bad mood and almost rabid. Khosrow Khan fled to the kitchen the moment he saw this.

I got out of the room on the east side overlooking the terrace. I saw Ziba chasing the chickens in the lower garden. All at once, he grabbed a fat chicken and moved to where he was tied before. Immediately, I grabbed a spade near the building and rushed towards him. As he was going back to his place from the end of the garden, I hit him with the spade to leave the chicken.

He did so, but then he jumped to the terrace and rushed towards me. It was so sudden that I didn't get the chance to push him away from me by the handle of the spade. Then he jumped on me with such power that I was knocked down to the ground and mildly bit my hand and arm a few times. It was as if he knew that he shouldn't badly hurt me even in his state of anger.

I screamed with pain and fear. Meanwhile, I saw Khosrow Khan standing motionless at the door of the kitchen, but he was so scared that he wouldn't come to rescue me from Ziba. I was left to myself, and Ziba finally released me due to my shouts and screams. He went back to his place and didn't bother the chickens anymore. It seemed that he'd realised that he'd done something wrong.

Crying, I passed by Khosrow Khan and went to the bathroom. There, I washed my hands and face and cleaned my clothes. After this incident, Ziba jumped on the wall and fled outside the garden. This was the right time for Khosrow Khan to hastily move the chickens back to their coops.

In the meantime, Ashraf and Siranoush arrived from grocery shopping on Pahlavi Street. Again at night, Ashraf called Mohammad by phone to return early to leash Ziba. I had minor injuries on my hand and arm caused by Ziba's bites which I disinfected with mercurochrome.

In the next few days, we noticed that the chickens had become sick, and we would lose them all if we didn't do anything about it. We had no choice but to slaughter them to eat. Mohammad constantly blamed himself for having bought them. We couldn't eat more than two chickens per day, so

Mohammad took some of them in his jeep to Sanam and Mahmoud, his mother and brother and Maryam, his sister. He also gave some others as gifts to his friends.

He kept the rest for Friday when he invited his friends and acquaintances, and we had a big party in the backyard. Helped by the friends' wives, Ashraf cooked pilaf and other meals for the guests to eat. Despite Mohammad's generosity and gift-giving, a small number of chickens and roosters perished.

On Saturday, Mohammad called a poultry farm from his office to come and get all their shelves. The chickens and roosters disappeared just as they had come. In the mornings, there was no more rooster to wake us up with its pleasant cock-a-doodle doo.

Ashraf began cleaning the building and terraces. Everywhere you looked, there was chicken droppings. Their poops in the lower garden were so much that Mohammad used them as fertiliser for flowers and trees. He gave them a little of it as he believed that the birds' droppings were very alkaline and strong and could hurt the delicate roots and stems of the trees and flowers.

Raising Pigeons in Our Home Garden; Ziba's Mischief

After we moved to Elahiyeh and settled there, my uncle "Ahmad" came there to visit us. He was very upset when I told him about the fate of our pigeons in the railway neighbourhood and that my father had given them all to one of the neighbours. He came to the rooftop with me and examined everything closely. Then he said: 'This is a very good place to keep pigeons.'

A few days after, he came to our house again in a car, with his friend Iraj, who was a strong and athletic man like himself. He was carrying a large cage in his hand with four nimble and young white pigeons in it. 'I've brought these for you,' he said. Their wings were tied so they would not fly. He continued: 'After four days, I will come and untie their wings. They'll get used to your house and the surroundings until then and will stay here.'

He'd also brought some millet for the pigeons. Then he left the pigeons in the stairway and told me: 'Leave them on the rooftop during the day to enjoy the sun and the wind.' A little later, he got into the car with Iraj and drove away.

In four days' time, he returned in the same car with Iraj, on a Friday afternoon. They went to the rooftop and saw the four pigeons perching together in a corner. Ahmad took them one by one and untied their wings. They gave them some millet and made them fly. He said: 'This is the right time for them to fly. They've got used to this place.'

The pigeons first jumped around the roof several times and slowly raised themselves. It was as if they were show pigeons, very good at jumping, because they were constantly increasing their height above the ground. Suddenly, we saw them accelerating so fast as if someone was following them. When they were about 200 metres above the roof, after a few more turnings, all four pigeons flew south towards the city. They disappeared from our sight in a few seconds.

Ahmad, Iraj and I were looking at this scene. We hoped the pigeons would return but to no avail. They were gone forever. Ahmad was very sad and upset. He told Iraj: 'We untied their wings too early. We should have left them tied for two more days.'

When Ahmad noticed how immensely sad I was, he promised to bring me four other pigeons. However, he didn't fulfil his promise due to too much work and the troubles he had.

It took Ahmad a year and a few months to come to us alone, on a Friday. He'd brought a large cage with four grey pigeons in it, with him. He said: 'These are very expensive pigeons. They belonged to a pigeon fancier who owed me some money. I got them instead of money. These are young and artistic doves that fly only at high altitudes.'

Then he tied their wings tightly, himself, to prevent them from flying and said: 'After at least six days, when they get used to this place, they should be untied to fly around the house, otherwise, they'll fly back to their previous owner.'

Mohammad told him: 'Had you brought these pigeons here earlier, we could have used the chicken coops for them, but now, I have to buy them a new cage.'

We'd given up raising our chickens in those days because they'd got sick. Ahmad took away the cage with him the next day because he'd borrowed it.

After he left, on the first day we kept the pigeons in Khosrow Khan's room so that Mohammad could buy a cage for them. Mohammad ordered a cage with an iron net around it which had no floor, to somebody near his office. They'd put a few sticks inside the cage so the pigeons could perch on. Mohammad brought the cage home from the city in his car and placed it in the upper garden, facing the southern terrace of the building. He also put a few bricks on both sides of the cage so it wouldn't be turned over by the wind. Inside the cage, he put a feed container for them on the floor.

On days when Ziba was tied, Khosrow Khan or I opened the cage door. The pigeons would get out and find their seed in the garden. At night, when we unleashed Ziba, I would return the pigeons to their nests. On the third day, after buying Sangak bread for breakfast, Khosrow Khan went to the pigeon cage to open the door and leave them in the garden. He rushed to the building and informed Ashraf and Mohammad that Ziba had devoured the pigeons and eaten some of them the night before when he was left free in the garden.

We all gathered around their cage and saw that the shameless dog had dug the ground in front of the cage and under it with his paws and entered their cage and killed them. Mohammad was amazed at Ziba's intelligence and constantly praised him. He seemed not to care much about the pigeons. However, the rest of the family was upset by this incident and

Ashraf repeatedly expressed her anger by saying: 'I ask God for forgiveness for this dog!'

This is how the pigeon-fancying story of Mohammad, Ahmad and I came to an end. I no longer had contact with any pigeons from then on.

Ziba's Fate

We treated Ziba crookedly, but she continued to harass our neighbours, especially the workers and farmers in our area. Everybody knew that we had a dog that was as dangerous as a wolf and were waiting for an excuse to keep it away from that area. Now Ziba was a perfect adult dog and needed a mate to walk around with every day. Chaining him during the day in that hot summer weather made him even more wild and savage.

One day, my cousin Mansour Vahedi came to see us. He was going to England for a course. Before leaving, he wanted to go to Rasht and then to Shaft (a city near Rasht) on a visit. He did not have more than a week to stay. Since I was on summer vacation, I took this opportunity and went with him.

When I returned, I heard that many things had happened in our absence. Mohammad's hand was in a bandage. He and Ashraf told me that Ziba tore her chain again, as usual, one day before noon, jumped off the wall to the other side and disappeared from sight. Then he came back home an hour later. He drank some water and ate the spleen which Mohammad had brought him the night before and jumped off the wall again and left.

Two hours later, about eight workers and brick layers gathered at our gate with shovels and pickaxes. They wanted to kill the dog because he had badly bitten the limbs and buttocks of two of their men. In the meantime, Ziba returned home and started running back and forth in the yard. Ashraf had told the workers from inside the building that they had no right to enter our house and she herself was afraid to come to the garden because Ziba might attack her too. But the workers called the police station and told them what was going on.

Three officers came to our house in a jeep with a hook mounted on the end of a long stick. They wanted to seize Ziba with the hook and take him with them or kill him. Meanwhile, Ziba jumped out of the wall again. Ashraf took the opportunity and immediately called Mohammad, thanks to Mehri from the English house, and told him the news. Mohammad asked my mother to ask the officers to wait for him to get home. He wanted to catch the dog himself. Then he immediately got in his jeep and headed home.

Half an hour later, Mohammad came hurriedly into the house. He saw that the officers had surrounded Ziba and tried to catch him by forcing his head into the hook with a long stick. Ziba also gathered himself, snored, showed his teeth and moved back and forth.

In the other hand of the officer, there was another baton to hit the dog on the head if he attacked. Seeing this situation, Mohammad shouted: 'Go away! Let him go. I will catch him myself.'

Mohammad was sure that Ziba's love for him would prevent him from attacking. So he approached Ziba without fear to put the collar around his neck and take him to his place. The angry dog, however, no longer knew him as a friend or acquaintance. He had spent many days wearing a collar in the hot summer weather without daily walks and affection. Being free and unleashed during nights and getting a little affection from Mohammad wasn't enough for him.

Captivity had turned him violent and rebellious. He leapt on Mohammad with a stride and bit his arm with his sharp teeth. Mohammad cried out in pain and pulled himself aside. Police officers attacked Ziba and wanted to shoot him, but Mohammad said in pain: 'Don't kill him! Just catch him!'

The officers finally managed to push his head into the hook.

Now we were faced with two problems; on the one hand, Mohammad's arm was bleeding, and he had to be given a tetanus injection and anti-rabies serum as soon as possible. And on the other, we had to know what they wanted to do with Ziba. They'd arrived in a jeep and didn't have a special vehicle or other means to take Ziba with them. Where could they take him, as the police station wasn't a place to keep the dogs?

Eventually, the officers decided again to shoot and kill the dog. Despite his pain, Mohammad told them that he'd take the dog to the city to the Animal Protection Organisation and hand him over to them. But he first wanted to be treated in the clinic in Tajrish. Two officers stayed at home to take care of Ziba.

The third one immediately took Mohammad to Tajrish in his jeep for treatment. After his injection and bandaging were done, they went back to the local police station to look for the address of the Animal Protection Organisation and then came back to our house with other equipment.

At 5 o'clock in the afternoon, they tied Ziba firmly to the back of Mohammad's jeep with the hook ring and a long stick. They covered Ziba's mouth with a muzzle mask to prevent him from biting. However, Mohammad sat behind the wheel of his jeep and drove Ziba behind the jeep towards the city. Ziba's situation with that hook ring, the long stick and that muzzle mask in that hot summer weather were depressing. Mohammad tried to drive very slowly so that Ziba could run alongside the car.

They entered Pahlavi Street from Fereshteh Street and moved towards the city. Ziba was running behind the jeep. Cars behind Mohammad's were all surprised to see this beautiful, yellow dog with a strong body and stretched ears being dragged so cruelly behind the car. They honked their horns to show their disapproval. Mohammad was not yet one kilometre from Amanieh station to the city when a large black American car stopped in front of his jeep.

An army officer got out of the car and stopped the jeep. Mohammad kept a few steps ahead of the black car. The army officer came to Mohammad and said angrily: 'Her Royal Highness, Ashraf Pahlavi, is in the car. She is very angry at your cruel act to tie the dog behind your car and severely harass it. She is the head of the Animal Protection Organisation, and this kind of treatment of animals is unbearable to her.'

Mohammad also stood firm in front of him and told him about Ziba's bite and the help of the police officers to catch him and that there was no other means to take the dog to the Animal Protection Organisation. He also showed his bandaged arm to the officer and finally added: 'If Her Royal

Highness knows of a better means to transfer this dog to the organisation, please let me know about it.'

The officer went back to Ashraf Pahlavi and, after a few words with her, pointed to Mohammad with his hand to continue his work and take Ziba to the organisation in that condition. Then he got in the black car and quickly drove away.

Two days after Ziba was handed over to the Animal Protection Organisation, Mohammad went there to visit him. He was kept in a solitary cage and started howling the moment he saw Mohammad, bumping himself against the wall of the cage and waving his tail. Mohammad's heart ached from all this affection and love.

'We checked,' said the head of the organisation. 'This is not a dog, but 100% a wolf. The person who sold it to you as a dog is a dishonest man. I'm afraid we have to kill this wolf with poison because keeping him is dangerous for the general public and even for you personally.'

Mohammad regretted that the organisation had no other way to keep that beautiful and perhaps rare wolf alive—or did not offer it to him. He could be given as a gift to the zoo, for example. The only benefit Ziba had for us was that no more thieves dared to come to our house again. He had scared the thieves of our region, and as long as we lived in Elahiyeh, no more thefts bothered us.

Mehri's Annoyance with Men

Mehri used to visit us like a family member and spend her leisure time with us because she had no one in Tehran except "Vazquez", her younger brother who lived in the city. She had no other relatives in Tehran. I had seen Vazquez several times in jeans which were a couple of sizes larger for him. He visited his sister on Thursday afternoons and stayed with her until Friday evening and carried his books with him. Apparently, she paid for his school expenses.

It was summer, and my cousin Nasser had come to see us from Rasht for two weeks. He was a primary school teacher in Rasht and a handsome, tall and slim young man who was also well-dressed. Mehri saw him in our house and liked him. Nasser was very sentimental and romantic, too. Seeing that beautiful girl, he immediately fell in love with her.

In Rasht, I had seen Nasser's poetry book at my aunt's, Seyyedeh Fattemeh, in which he had written a collection of the most beautiful poems about love and romance with a flower or a nice scenery drawn next to each. Nasser and Mehri were attracted to see each other like magnets. Our house was not a place for lovemaking, and going out as a couple also caused suspicion. So Nasser always took me out with them to show that we were wandering in those hills. Poor lovers could do nothing else.

At times, when Mehri was overwhelmed by emotions, she had tears in her eyes. I think the only thing she did at a young age was just work. She needed love and affection. When the two of them were talking, I turned my face away from them and got away a few metres to let them be at ease together. After a while of talking to each other, their enthusiasm and warmth subsided and we all returned home.

Two weeks of staying at our house passed very quickly. Nasser had to return to Rasht because his school was starting. I no longer know what happened between Mehri and Nasser. All I know is that Nasser had just started his teaching career and was still unable to start a family. And also because he, himself, was very busy studying to get his teaching degree.

Mehri was also living her life in the house of that English couple and their children. She had to earn her own living and support her brother with the money she received from them and perhaps send financial aid to her family in the province, too. Mehri said goodbye to Nasser with tears in her eyes.

Almost three years later in December 1960, I heard at lunch from Nasser, who had come to Tehran to Keyvan's house, that Mehri had visited him shortly after his return to Rasht to encourage him to marry her. Apparently, Nasser was not ready to start a family due to work, school and financial problems, and he could not promise her anything. He honestly told her about his situation, and after a while, their relationship cooled down due to the distance and then ended.

Sometimes, if Mehri had a day off on a Thursday afternoon, she would go to the city (Tehran) and make an appointment with her brother Vazquez to see each other in

Mohammad's office and return to Elahiyeh at night in his jeep. At that time, Mohammad had a secretary in his office named Ali Aqa, who was a 23-year-old, tall and slim young man with a boney face. He was a sympathetic and charming young man whose only thought was to attract girls. The way I saw it, he was very successful in doing so, because he won the hearts of the girls with a sweet smile and loving look.

He was almost as tall as Nasser and even looked like him. He smiled his way and was very attractive. Entering Mohammad's office, Mehri was surprised at his similarity with Nasser. She felt like she was standing before him and remembered her lost love. She thought that Ali Aqa would also be similar to Nasser in character; pure, honest and polite.

The same night, she wrote a letter to Ali Aqa and told him that meeting and talking to him had impressed her so much, and she asked him to see her again. She gave the letter to her brother to deliver to Ali Aqa on Saturday after school. As I was later told by Ali Aqa, himself, he welcomed Mehri's request and they met each other a couple of times in the city. Mehri, then, invited him to go to her place when Linda and Martin and their children were out. Ali Aqa told me about the nice time he had with Mehri and the delicious meals she cooked for him. She also ironed her shirt and suit, but wouldn't let him touch her before marriage.

The last night, as they were warmly speaking to each other, the sound of Martin's car horn was heard calling for Mehri to open the large gate of the house. Ali Aqa hurriedly gathered his belongings and ran to jump from the east wall of the building to the wasteland behind it and disappeared in the dark of the night. Mehri didn't hear from him anymore. Apparently, Ali Aqa had found somebody else.

Mehri was sad and depressed for a few weeks and sometimes cried involuntarily. In response to my mother's questions who kept asking her for the reason, she said it didn't matter, but I knew that it was because Ali Aqa had left her for good. I kept her secret to myself, and my mother never got to know the cause of Mehri's grief.

Four years later, I saw Mehri buying ice cream for an almost three-year-old boy, and they were coming out of the shop. I didn't show myself to her, but I was very happy to see Mehri and her son because now I knew that she was finally having a family with her husband and child.

Mohammad Planting Poppies in Our Residential Garden

Our gardener, Hossein Aqa, had told Mohammad that he had planted poppies in his hometown of Kuhdasht, in Lorestan. He asked Mohammad to let him do it there, too. He added: 'It's a lucrative business.'

Mohammad gave him permission, and Hossein Aqa planted poppies in a large area, at the end of the garden. The idea of planting poppies was suggested earlier to Mohammad by his friend, Jalal Farazi who'd told him: 'You have a house and a garden in a remote area from the city, on a main street which is ideal for growing opium.'

Following his visit to Zomorodian's chicken coop, where he'd taken advantage of every metre of his place, Mohammad constantly thought about making the best of his garden. Thus, he thought planting poppies at the bottom of the garden in that remote area, hidden from the sight of the people, was trouble-free and financially worthwhile. In addition, Mohammad himself was a smoker and thought that by growing poppies, he would get good quality opium and save himself from the fake opium in which everything was added.

It was Monday, 9 June 1958. The bell at the end of the lesson at "Safa ye Esfahani" school rang. I headed home. I passed the last corner of Fereshteh Street. In the distance, I saw an army jeep standing next to our house, and its top was full of poppy flowers that Mohammad had planted in our garden. When I got close to our house, I saw a policeman holding Mohammad's two opium pipes, before he got into a jeep.

I was heartbroken. My heart started pounding. I entered the house with fear, trembling. I saw six or seven guards inside the garden and outside the house, moving around. I was shocked and terrified.

As I entered the building, I saw Ashraf lying on her bed in the first room, to the left of the hall, holding my sister Houri, who was just a few days old. She looked pale with fear. Nanneh Jan was sitting next to her on the bed, comforting her, although she, herself, was very much scared. The gardener, Hossein Aqa, was standing outside the building watching the guards calmly. He could have been feeling guilty for encouraging my father to grow poppies.

Meanwhile, the police left our house on foot or in jeep. There was only one constable left who wore a special suit. He was a tall and slim young man, about 34 years old, who looked very kind. He tried to calm us down with his warm tone. He constantly comforted Ashraf, who was crying at times. He told her: 'Don't be upset ma'am. No crime has taken place here. Guards have just found poppy bushes before they had fruits. God willing, your husband arrives and clarifies the matter.'

From what he was saying, I concluded that he was there to arrest the felon, Mohammad, the moment he arrived. Siranush arrived in half an hour. Seeing our distress, she also got scared. With a lump in her throat, she went to Ashraf and stayed close to her.

Photo No. 28: Siranush, at the age of 11 (1958).

Kourosh was also moving around us, not knowing what was going on. In the meantime, Nanneh Jan got into the kitchen and started cooking lunch for us. It was noon time, and the children were hungry. In that mishmash, she cooked a delicious "Mirza Qassemi" with pilaf for us and served us a nice meal.

The constable told Ashraf that he was going home for lunch, but would come back to us in the afternoon. He so introduced himself to my mother: 'Constable, Molavi, from Tajrish police station.'

He might have meant the police station in Dezashib, but he served in its branch on Amanieh Street. His house was near Amanieh Street. He gave his phone number to Ashraf, but we couldn't call him, because we didn't have a telephone at home.

At lunch, Ashraf told me and Siranush about what had happened that morning, in detail. She said: 'Ms Arsanjani had come to our house at nine o'clock, together with a civil engineer.'

My father had pledged all his garden house with Ms Arsanjani, due to his insecure financial situation, at 30,000 Tumans, while its value was in fact 150000 Tumans. It was time to repay the amount, but Mohammad had no money to give it to her. So Ms Arsanjani threatened to sue him.

Finally, with the sum added to the interest, Ms Arsanjani tried to win the house as well as the garden by conducting an auction. The gate was open, so they got in and stood in front of it, calling for Mohammad. As Mohammad was not at home at that time, Ms Arsanjani asked the engineer to measure the garden house and determine its area.

My mother did not allow Ms Arsanjani to come further inside the house garden. She said to her: 'Our master is not at home and a stranger has no right to enter it.'

After hearing this, Ms Arsanjani put her hands on her waist and said: 'This house is mine now. I will decide what to do with it.'

They were arguing when Ms Arsanjani's eyes fell on the poppy bushes to the south of the garden. She looked at them carefully and shouted: 'Now you are also growing poppies in my garden. I will show you what I'll do.' Then she turned to the engineer and said, 'You see that these people are producing drugs in my house.' Turning to Ashraf, she said: 'Now I will show you what I'll do next.' Then to the engineer: 'Let's go to the police station and from there contact the anti-narcotics department and inform them about these.'

Ms Arsanjani and the engineer left. Planting poppies was banned at that time. Laws have been strictly enforced since the time of Ahmad Qavam, nicknamed Qavam al-Saltaneh (1942).

Half an hour later, seven or eight policemen came by jeep to inspect, but since they did not have a warrant to enter the house, they went from the wall of the house to the rooftop to watch the traffic until the order requested by the court arrived. Despite her weakness, Ashraf rushed to Mehri Khanum, the maid of the English family and asked her to call Mohammad. Mehri Khanum did so, and Mohammad immediately sent his secretary, Ali Aqa, to our house to remove all the poppy bushes from the garden and throw them behind the wall of the house. Ali Aqa was a sympathetic and loving young man who had won the love of Mehri Khanum. He always wore a grey suit; it seemed as if he didn't have anything more.

After half an hour, Ali Aqa came to our house in a car. The moment he entered the house, he went to the garden and began to uproot the poppy bushes. He would then pick them up and throw them behind the wall of our house, to the east. The guards, who were watching on the roof of the house, shouted at him to stop. They even threw a few bricks at him from behind the roof to stop him from digging up the bushes, but he ignored their words and threats and continued with his work.

Ali Aqa had uprooted more than half of the bushes and thrown them behind the wall when the court ordered them to enter the house and search for drugs. The guards immediately entered the house from the rooftop. The first thing they did was slap Ali Aqa, but he ignored it and wanted to continue with his work. When he was threatened with arrest, he stopped working and told the police: 'You only have the right to record the same number of plants in the garden into your protocol. The lady of the house and other members (she meant Nanneh Jan and Hossein Aqa, our gardener) are witnesses.'

They asked him: 'What are you doing here?'

He replied: 'I am a family friend.'

Officers ate all the strawberries we had planted while cutting the poppies. There was nothing left of them.

Guards had seen from the rooftop that Ashraf was very weak, and she could hardly move due to her recovery. In particular, they had seen Nanneh Jan grab her arm as she walked, so she would not fall. As a result, Ashraf was resting in her room when they stormed into the house, after receiving a court order. Next to Ashraf's room, the guards told Nanneh Jan: 'We will not enter this room, because the lady of the house needs to rest with her baby.'

They started looking for drugs in the kitchen, which was the first room after entering the building. Nanneh Jan took the opportunity to place two of Mohammad's opium pipes and other smoking devices, such as needles, sticks and a few grams of opium, under Ashraf's pillow. After the police searched all the rooms and found nothing, they knocked on

Ashraf's room. They said: 'Now it is the turn of the housewife's room.'

Nanneh Jan protested: 'My granddaughter is sick and has just given birth.'

But they turned a deaf ear to what she said and entered the room. They went straight to Ashraf's bed. It was as if they already had enough experience and knew that everything was hidden under the head of a sick or hospitalised person. They easily found two opium pipes and their accessories, with a very small amount of opium and took them with them. In response to their question about who the one in charge of planting, and the owner of the opium pipes, was, Ashraf introduced Mohammad as she couldn't do anything else. They took his address to go to him.

I started studying my lessons after lunch. A couple of hours later, the constable showed up again. He was accompanied by his wife. She was a medium-sized woman, about 160 cm. tall, wearing a floral pattern pale red dress with a white strap sewn around her chest.

She had black, polished shoes with heels of 2 cm and was a neat-looking lady around 30 years old. The moment she saw Ashraf, she began to comfort her and said that her husband had told her about the incident after he'd come back home. She said that she was very sorry about what had happened to us and that she'd come to see Ashraf and us, the children. She further added that her husband promises to do whatever he can for us.

According to this lady, they lived at the end of Amanieh Hill in the south, close to Pahlavi Road. There was only Amanieh Hill separating us. They sat in the hall for a while. Then, as they were leaving, my mother, Nanneh Jan and all of us stood outside on the terrace on the south side of the building.

The constable and his wife talked about everything to alleviate our shock and anxiety and comfort us. After saying goodbye, it was decided that the next day, that kind couple would come to us again. Then they left.

Ashraf wondered why the constable was so kind to us. It occurred to me that maybe he expected a reward from Mohammad, or he was told to be kind to this kind of family in such situations to alleviate their shock. Or, they might have been naturally kind people. I changed my dress after they left and got ready to go to Mohammad's office to see what we had to do next.

To my surprise, every time I saw a policeman on the way, I was scared and my arms and legs started shaking. I was in a state of hysteria. I felt that the policeman could arrest me, and I wanted to run away from him. But in fact, the constable, or constables, were so engaged in their own work, or in talking to their co-workers, that they did not pay any attention to me at all. It seemed to me that perhaps the shock of what had happened that day had a profound psychological effect on me. Seeing the officers and their uniforms terrified me.

There was only Ali Aqa in Mohammad's office. When he saw me, he said: 'It is good that you came. I was coming to you, myself.' He continued: 'Several officers came and took your father with them. It was afternoon.

'They knocked on the door after lunch. I saw through the keyhole that three people, one in plain clothes and two guards, were standing in front of the door. I told your father about it. He immediately opened the last door of the room and went here. I closed the door on him. He told me to tell the officers that Mr So-and-so wasn't there.'

Mohammad's office was located in a building on Shah Reza Street (now the Islamic Revolution), approximately 50 metres away from Pahlavi Street (now Valiasr), facing the Shahrdari Cafe (Student Park). As I climbed the narrow steps of the building, I came to Mohammad's office on the first floor. It was the first room on the right-hand side of the corridor. The sign on its door read: 'Money Office.'

When you entered the room, there was a female secretary's desk, and on the other side, there was a male secretary with a few chairs for the clients. The room led to a second room, which belonged to Mohammad, as the head of the office. The second room also opened to a third room which was closed, because Mohammad had rented it to a dentist. In front of the door of the third room, they'd placed a very large sofa for three people; this closed its entry to the third room.

Ali Aqa continued: 'I opened the door. Three officers came in. In response to their question about your father, I said: "Mr Pourkian, whom you are looking for, is not here now. He went for lunch this afternoon and told me that he wouldn't return to the office today. You can see him tomorrow morning."'

The officers and the one in plain clothes looked around. They saw me in the first room, and there was nobody in the second room. They came out and saw that the corridor led to a door with the sign "Dr Rasoul Mousavi, Dentist" written on it. The office was closed because it was not working hours. So they went back to the first room.

The officer in plain clothes got into the second room. He looked around a little, then he ordered the other two officers to remove the large sofa in front of the door of the third room. They moved the sofa and the door of the third room was opened. They got into the room. It was the dentist's waiting room.

There they saw Mohammad lying comfortably on a chair, reading a book. The officers themselves were surprised at what they saw there. Before they could say a word, Mohammad asked: 'You're looking for something?'

The man in plain clothes said: 'Yes. Please come with us.'

When Mohammad went with them, he asked them where they were taking him. They said: 'We are currently taking you to the temporary detention centre of the judiciary in Toupkhaneh' so that our colleagues can take you to court tomorrow for interrogation and trial. At this time, Mohammad immediately ordered me to go back home, bring him a blanket, a pillow, house clothes, a razor, toothpaste and a toothbrush and something to eat for the night. It was as if he knew what awaited him in the detention centre.

Ali Aqa and I went home. Meanwhile, he told me about going to our house and removing the poppies in the garden. Ashraf, with the help of Nanneh Jan, prepared everything according to Mohammad's order and gave it to Ali Aqa. We walked all that way back to Pahlavi Street again. There, we got in a car, got off at Shah Reza crossroads and took a taxi to Toupkhaneh (now Imam Khomeini Square).

We found the detention centre by asking the passers-by. It was located on the west-hand side of Toupkhaneh. As we entered Toupkhaneh From Sepah Street (now Imam Khomeini Street), just 50 metres to the right of Sepah Street, there was a building with a high wall and an iron gate, in front of which one or two officers in military uniform were on duty.

Ali Aqa told the officer in front of the detention centre the name "Mohammad Pourkian" and continued that he had brought him his sleeping and food items and wanted to give them to him. We entered a room overlooking the courtyard and waited for them to call Mohammad and bring him to us. Everyone was standing or walking in the yard of the detention centre. There was no place for sitting. The courtyard was full of criminals.

Most of them were taxi drivers and car owners who either had an accident and got away without a driver's licence or had not paid their government fine. Other offenders included all classes of people, including drug addicts and those convicted of fraud, beatings and sex abuse.

In the midst of that criminal crowd, I saw Mohammad from afar. He did not look at all like he had been charged with drug possession. He'd gathered people around himself and was telling stories to them. Everyone listened intently to what he had to say. Finally, an officer called him.

I saw him coming to us. We gave him the items he had ordered, wrapped in a sheet by Ashraf. Then he pulled Ali Aqa to a corner and told him that he was to be taken to court the next morning by the investigator. He asked Ali Aqa to go to the court of narcotics branch to "Mr Torbati" early in the morning, before anything was done, and confess that he himself had planted all the poppy plants in the garden of Fereshteh Street, and those opium pipes and the opium belonged to him. He told him to say he was responsible for everything, and Mr Pourkian was innocent.

If Ali Aqa was caught, Mohammad could get out of prison, but if Mohammad was convicted, no one could save him from prison and the "Money Office" would be closed. As a result, he would lose his job and be unemployed. In addition, for this service and kind act, Mohammad would give him an extra sum of money later on.

There I noticed that the face of Ali Aqa, who was thin and looked more like an opium addict, was more acceptable in court than anyone else. Ali Aqa started saying yes, yes, I will do whatever you say. Then Mohammad turned to me and asked what had happened at home during that time.

I told him about the officer and his wife. Mohammad asked me to tell Ashraf that the next day, or the day after it, everything would be fine and he'd come back home. We came out of the gate of the detention centre. I said goodbye to Ali Aqa and headed home.

The next afternoon, the officer came to us again with his wife. They behaved so kindly that it seemed like they knew us for many years. The officer explained a little about his work and said that theft was more common in their neighbourhood because affluent and wealthy families lived in that area. He and his constables were always involved in robberies in the area, but so far he had not had a case of drugs or poppy cultivation. My mother talked a little about the thieves who almost stripped our house at night and the carelessness of the guards who did not patrol our neighbourhood at night, which further motivated the theft.

His wife also told my mother that she sewed for several tailors at home, and although they didn't have a child then, they planned to have one. The couple were really sympathetic and tried to reduce our fears and excitement about that unforeseen event. After a while, they said goodbye and left us, and we never saw them again or heard anything from them.

Three days later, on Thursday, 12 June 1958, Mohammad came home at night. His eyes looked tired as if he had been badly treated in the detention centre. One could not expect anything else from him. The detention centre had only one toilet. There was no food, no tea, no water to have and no place to sleep.

There was nothing. They had given the criminals a bare yard to spend the night before being taken to the court the next day, to clarify their case. It was cold at night and difficult to stay in that open air without clothes, beddings and food. In fact, it was a precautionary measure by the authorities to let the felons know what awaited them if they committed another crime.

If someone had money, he would give it to one of the constables to get something for him outside, or ask his family to bring him something from home; otherwise, he would have a hard time there in the yard. Now Mohammad was lucky that we had taken some necessities to him. In addition, he had money with him to get by. He constantly damned Jalal Farazi, his friend, for causing him that trouble.

According to Mohammad, Ali Aqa had actually gone to the relevant investigator and confessed that he was Mr Pourkian's gardener and had planted the poppies. He told them: 'My employer is innocent.'

As a result of his confession, Mohammad was released. They made a case in the name of Ali Aqa. There was no other choice.

They sent it to the court. There, they asked for a financial guarantee of 5,000 Tumans to release Ali Aqa until the time of his trial. Mohammad immediately brought the document and gave a guarantee of 5,000 Tumans to release Ali Aqa from the temporary prison of the judiciary. Then he called the officers who had come to our house and complained about the situation that they had created for us.

They said: 'We are innocent. That lady was the one who caused this situation for you and reported you.'

Mohammad gave them 200 Tumans to change the questions and write a new report for a new file for Ali Aqa. In it, they wrote that a small amount of poppy had grown among the flower seeds. Mohammad had already told them: 'What if the poppy seeds were mixed with the seeds of the flowers? It wouldn't do anything with us then.'

Ali Aqa signed the report case. The new case was sent back to the court. The court was convened and Ali Aqa was acquitted. In this way, Mohammad released Ali Aqa from prison by bribing this and that and manipulating the case. And he, himself, also got rid of the court.

I heard the rest of the story from my aunt, Iran. She said: 'It was near sunset, on a Wednesday, when Mohammad and Ali Aqa went to Sanam and Mahmoud's house, on Farvardin Street, Teimuri Alley. It was located on the right-hand side of Giti Lane. Mohammad asked Sanam to cook something for them while they took a bath. Then they sat at the table to eat their dinner, like two princes, together with Mahmoud who'd just returned from work.

'Sanam placed warm and cosy bedding for Ali Aqa on the first floor. The next morning, a royal breakfast awaited Mohammad and Ali Aqa, too. They all had their breakfast and went to work with Mahmoud.'

Mahmoud looked for his watch after getting dressed. Wherever he searched, he did not find it. He told the story to Sanam. Sanam commented: 'This is the work of this fellow that Mohammad brought with him.' The place of the watch was known, and Mahmoud always put it on the table before going to bed as usual.

Sanam pulled Mohammad aside and said to him: 'Tell your clerk, without anyone knowing to lose his face, to put the watch on the table and then leave.'

Mohammad was very upset that his mother suspected his secretary. To him, his secretary was an innocent person. Secondly, it was not good to convict a guest of theft. However, Sanam wasn't convinced and didn't care about what he said. She said: 'My son, Mahmoud, is sewing all day long to earn his living. Now your secretary has stolen his watch.'

With no more talks, Sanam, herself, went straight to Ali Aqa and told him: 'My son's watch is missing. I want to search your pockets.'

Ali Aqa resisted a little, but Sanam searched his pockets without waiting for his answer. She found Mahmoud's watch in one of his pockets and gave it back to Mahmoud. Mohammad later complained: 'This thief embarrassed me before my mother. Then at the office, he asked for more money and credit for his help. He expected more and more every day. So I fired him and kicked him out of my office.'

Mohammad's engagement with the poppy report took him three to four days and cost him 200–300 Tumans. Once he got rid of the poppy problem, he went after Ms Arsanjani and sent her this message: 'If you meant to harass me, I know how to do the same to you. I'll make you follow suit for three to four years. Do you think I'll give you the money? Now start!'

There was a man named "Hossein Zargari" whom Mohammad paid 10 Tumans to follow the file and get it from the archives and read it. He put it under his arm and took it out with him. Ms Arsanjani kept going to the "Executive Office" and requested her case. The archivist told her: 'Ma'am! We do not know to whom we sent the file. Wait a little more for it to be found.'

Mohammad made Ms Arsanjani run after the case for a while, even though she was a smart woman. Her father, Colonel Arsanjani, worked in the police force as "chief accountant". Ms Arsanjani thought that because her father was a colonel, she could auction off the house and garden.

'Over my dead body, Madam,' Mohammad told her.

He set to work at once and mortgaged the house to a benevolent man named Haji Safari, who lived in Shemiran and really wanted to help us. He gave his money to Ms Arsanjani and thus embarrassed her. Haji Safari had a Chelokababi shop on Tajrish Square. It seems that Mohammad knew him in Chelokababi because he mostly ate there with his friends and was considered one of his good customers.

Mohammad's Haste in Migrating from Elahiyeh

There was talk about building the third Shemiran Road, beginning in March 1955. According to the municipal plan, this road was to be drawn from the north of "Bahar Street" to "Elahiyeh-Davoudieh" and then lead to two streets, one part to the old Shemiran Road (now Shariati Street) and the other near Amanieh Hill to Pahlavi Road (Valiasr). It was seven kilometres long and 120 metres wide and had three large squares. The passage of this road through Elahiyeh also included our house garden.

The construction of this road was criticised by some because they believed that the budget could be spent on more emergency plans. The program was also postponed for some time due to its crossing through the "Motor Regiment" in "Abbas Abad" (now Shahid Beheshti Street).[18]

Mohammad's concerns were somehow relieved. One night, however, he informed us that they planned to construct a road, 60 m. wide, in Elahiyeh which was the continuation of Abbas Abad Street, coming from the city, towards Tajrish.

---

[18] Ettela'at newspaper; 14 March 1955, 5 April, 12 June, 30 July, 26 Aug., 7, 13 September and 10 October 1956.

"Lotfollah Tarqi" sent Mohammad to the municipality, by prior appointment, to see the map of that street. Mohammad saw that our house garden fell right in the middle of the street.

Oh my God! Lotfollah had frightened Mohammad. Soon after, Mohammad rushed to find a customer to sell the house to as soon as possible. One evening, the famous singer "Delkash" (Esmat Baqerpour Baboly) came to see our house in her blue and white American car, "A Ford Edsel". I was so pleasantly surprised by this visit that I immediately memorised the number "218" of her car.

She was a very short woman wearing high-heeled shoes. However, she still looked short despite her shoes. She liked the house. Mohammad sold the house to her for less than 100,000 Tumans. He was very upset because he thought he had no choice but to sell his house.

He believed that Delkash could fight the municipality better. But after the intervention of the Fakhr al-Dowleh family, who were very influential, and the direct influence of Dr Ali Amini, Mrs Fakhr al-Dowleh's son, the municipal plan changed, and they prevented the street from being blocked in that area and diverted it to another direction. Therefore, neither our house nor Mrs Fakhr al-Dowleh's property was hurt.

Photo No. 29: The news of the construction cancellation of the third road in Ettela'at newspaper (Wednesday, 17 April 1963).

Mohammad hurried a lot to sell the house. In that way, we had to move from Elahiyeh to a house in the city on "Keivan Street", "Simetri area" (now Kargar Street). But instead, we children were able to breathe among the people again and enjoy living with them after five years of being away from the city and living in isolation in Elahiyeh.

However, Mohammad was still dreaming about his former house in Elahiyeh. Sometime later, in a deal, he acquired a 1,000 square metres of land, almost 200 metres above our previous building, worth 60,000 Tumans. One day when he was a guest at his mother Sanam, he started showing off and sweetening himself. He said to her: 'Mother! I've finally bought a 1,000-metre garden near my former home.'

Mahmoud, his brother who was also present there, asked: 'How much did you buy it for, brother?'

Mohammad said: '60 Tumans per square metre.'

Mahmoud asked: 'Could you give it to me? You are familiar with land transactions and can buy something similar for yourself again.'

When Sanam saw her younger son's interest in the land, she pressured Mohammad to give the land to his brother, Mahmoud! Loving his mother dearly, Mohammad agreed. He said: 'This land is yours. Just let me first ask the notary to write the deed for you to sign.'

The way Mohammad told this to me, I think he gave the land as a gift to his brother. I never found out if he got any money from Mahmoud or spared it generously as a gift. Mahmoud later built a temporary villa on the land with two 30- and 20-square-metre rooms, where Mohammad was later forced to live in for some time, due to his bankruptcy. Mahmoud then demolished it and built a stylish building there for himself and lived there with his family.

Photo No. 30: Taken from the ridge of Amanieh Hill. Mahmoud's temporary villa with a few apple and cherry trees, as well as grape vines in the front row, following several incomplete buildings on the right. Fereshteh Street can be seen from the left side of the trees to the east. The street in front is the former Vojdani Street (now Bidar), located behind Amanieh Hill (24 May1968).